★

CONTENTS

Introduction   4

Breakfast   ● 9

Soups and Salads   ● 42

Snacks and Light Lunches   ● 78

Dinner and Sides   ● 124

Desserts   ● 166

Drinks   ● 204

Index   222

INTRODUCTION

You hear a lot of talk about low sugar these days, but it can be confusing. In this cookbook, bursting with 150 delicious recipes for day-to-day living, we've taken a simple approach and the recipes you'll find here are based on three easy principles: avoiding refined white sugar, reducing overall sugar consumption and experimenting with alternatives.

AVOIDING WHITE SUGAR

Why avoid refined white sugar? Excessive sugar consumption can cause type 2 diabetes and obesity, both big problems in the Western world. It's the fructose molecule found in refined sugar (and other sugars) that's to blame. The body can't process too much fructose, and it quickly turns to fat in the liver, causing diabetes, heart disease and other health problems. Glucose, on the other hand, is metabolised by all the cells in our body. To make matters worse, our brains are intensely receptive to sugar, making it hard to find the off switch when reaching for that extra chocolate biscuit.

REDUCING OVERALL SUGAR CONSUMPTION

The average Australian, Brit or American consumes in the region of 27 teaspoons of sugar a day. With the World Health Organization recommending 5 teaspoons a day, it's clear we have work to do to cut back. The good news is that this book will help you do it, it's not as hard as you might think, and you can still eat cake! You'll find that some recipes in this book do include sugar of some kind, maybe coconut sugar or honey, or even just the natural stuff that comes from fruit. Fruit contains important vitamins and nutrients and one to two pieces a day are good for you. It's a case of everything in moderation.

UNDERSTANDING THE ALTERNATIVES

There are plenty of sugar substitutes and sweeteners on the market these days, so how do you know which to choose? Here is an overview the alternatives we recommend in the recipes in this book, plus a few tips to help you to substitute in other recipes.

Stevia

Stevia is a natural herb that is processed for use in cooking as a powder or liquid. It's very sweet, but it is 100% fructose free, making it the preferred choice of sweetener for many low sugar cooks. One teaspoon of liquid stevia equates to one tablespoon of powdered stevia which equals a cup of old-fashioned sugar. Got that? Don't worry, in this book we provide the exact measurements of stevia that you need, but you can always substitute in other recipes if you bear that equation in mind.

Erythritol

Despite it's scientific-sounding name, erythritol is a naturally occurring nectar in plants, and fruits and vegetables like grapes and mushrooms. It's a good choice when looking for a direct substitute for sugar as it measures the same cup for cup.

Natvia

Natvia is a natural sweetener made by combining the purest and sweetest parts of the stevia plant and erythritol. Natvia is fructose free. It can be used as a direct substitute for sugar.

Coconut sugar

A sustainable option made from the sap of the coconut palm, coconut sugar is nutritious and has a low GI, which means no sugar high and lows. But it does have a fructose content on a par with honey and white sugar, so don't overdo it. Coconut sugar can be used as a direct substitute for sugar.

Maple syrup
The sugary sap from the maple tree is delicious, but it contains about 40% fructose, so use in moderation. Maple syrup can replace regular sugar as and when you need it.

Honey
Honey is made up of around 75% sugar (glucose and fructose equally). It has more calories than sugar but because it's sweeter you can use less of it. Choose honey that's been organically produced to reap the full benefits, such as antioxidant and antibacterial properties. Consider using different flavours of honey in your cooking for variety.

Honey and maple syrup are sweeter than sugar, so if you're substituting for sugar in a recipe, use three quarters of a cup for each cup of sugar. You'll also need to decrease the liquid requirement in the recipe by three tablespoons per cup.

If baking with honey or maple syrup, reduce the oven temperature by 15°C (25°F), since maple syrup and honey caramelise and burn faster than granulated sweeteners.

Rice malt syrup (also known as brown rice syrup)
Made from boiling brown rice, rice malt syrup is gluten and wheat free. It has a mild butterscotch flavour and can be used as a condiment as well as a sugar substitute in cooking. It is 100% fructose free. It can be used as a direct substitute for sugar or honey.

WHAT ELSE CAN YOU DO?
Understanding sugar and sugar substitutes is key to a low sugar diet, but there are some other steps you can take that will have a positive impact too.

Switch your choice of carbohydrates
If you want to minimise your sugar intake it's best to eliminate or reduce

simple carbohydrates – such as white bread, pasta and rice – as these foods have a high GI and promote an insulin-spike response. Shift to wholegrain breads, grain products and brown rice instead as they have higher fibre content meaning absorption is slower and there is less of an insulin response. Look for foods that have at least 3g of fibre per 100 calories.

Check the label

Be vigilant about the food you buy, especially pre-made sauces, marinades and dressings and other packaged or processed foods. Most contain sugar. In this book, you'll find easy recipes to make your own sauces, dressings and mayonnaise. Use them and you'll be free from the chore of constantly checking labels.

Buy unsweetened

Look for the unsweetened variations of common foods that you use, such as cocoa, almond milk and peanut butter.

A word about fruit

Remember the days when we were urged to eat more fruit? Now it seems we're being told to eat less, or less of certain fruits anyway. If you are really keen to understand the relative sugar content of different fruits, do your homework. Otherwise, be aware that some fruits are sweeter than others. On the high-sugar (eat less) side are bananas, watermelon, grapes, mangos and figs, among others, and on the low-sugar (eat more) side are blueberries and raspberries, kiwi fruit and pears, among others. Also be mindful of dried fruits. These do tend to contain a lot of sugar, especially cranberries. If you love them, keep an eye out for the variety sweetened with fruit juice, consider making your own, or just enjoy in moderation.

The good news is that once you've got a handle on these basic principles, low-sugar cooking is easy – and inclusive too. Cake, desserts, biscuits, meat, fish, pasta, pizza, potatoes, cheese, butter, yoghurt, fruit and, of course, vegetables are all on the menu, and you'll find lots of inspirational ideas for how to prepare them in this book.

BREAKFAST

Hearty quinoa with baked eggs 10

Coconut mango Chia seed pudding 12

Stuffed Omelette with spinach and cheese 13

Homemade granola 14

Scrambled tofu on toast 16

Roasted fennel cherry tomatoes 18

Avocado scrambled egg wraps 19

Chia berry pots with lavender honey 20

Protein muffins 22

Asparagus frittata 23

Omelette with mushrooms 24

Coconut mango rice pudding 26

Grilled sardines with lemon 27

Red quinoa with apples 28

Egg baked in avocado 30

Coco-cashew nut butter 31

Whole wheat blackberry pancakes 32

Blueberry yoghurt pot 34

Overnight oatmeal 35

Florentine eggs 36

Quinoa porridge bowl 38

Cinnamon rice porridge 39

Poached egg with spinach 40

HEARTY QUINOA WITH BAKED EGGS

INGREDIENTS

2 cups (500ml, 1pt) vegetable or chicken stock

1 cup (170g, 6oz) quinoa

2 tbsps olive oil

4-6 mushrooms, chopped

1 red capsicum, diced

10 cherry tomatoes

2 cloves garlic, minced

Zest of 1 lemon

Salt and pepper, to taste

2 eggs

Fresh parsley, to garnish

METHOD

1. Bring stock to the boil in an ovenproof medium frying pan (or shallow baking dish).

2. Add quinoa, reduce heat and simmer for 15 minutes, until cooked. Fluff with a fork and set aside.

3. Heat oil in a saucepan and cook mushrooms and capsicum over a low heat for 5 minutes.

4. Add tomatoes and fry for 2 minutes, until charred. Add garlic and cook, stirring, for a further 2 minutes.

5. Preheat the oven to 180°C (350°F, Gas Mark 4).

6. Add lemon zest and cooked quinoa and stir through. Season to taste with salt and pepper.

7. Crack eggs into the middle of the pan on top of the quinoa. Transfer the pan to the oven and bake for 10 minutes until eggs whites are just set and yolks are still runny.

8. Garnish with parsley and black pepper, to serve.

COCONUT MANGO CHIA PUDDING

INGREDIENTS

1 cup (250ml, 8fl oz) coconut milk

3 tbsps chia seeds

2 tbsps honey or maple syrup

½ tsp vanilla extract

½ mango, diced

METHOD

1. In a jar or mixing bowl, combine coconut milk, chia seeds, honey or syrup and vanilla.

2. Cover with plastic wrap and chill in fridge for 15 minutes to allow chia to absorb and swell.

3. Remove and stir to thoroughly combine and then return to fridge for at least 2 hours.

4. Remove from fridge and divide mixture evenly into serving glasses.

5. Serve topped with mango pieces.

STUFFED OMELETTE WITH SPINACH AND CHEESE

INGREDIENTS

1 egg

3 egg whites

1 tbsp Parmesan cheese, grated

1 tbsp cheddar cheese, grated

¼ tsp salt

⅛ tsp chilli flakes (optional)

Pinch of ground nutmeg

Pinch of black pepper

Olive oil, for frying

¼ onion, very finely chopped

1 bunch baby spinach, leaves picked (reserve a few leaves for garnish)

METHOD

1. Whisk together egg and egg whites in a bowl.

2. Add Parmesan and cheddar cheeses, salt, chilli flakes, if using nutmeg and pepper and mix well to combine.

3. Heat oil in a frying pan over a medium heat, saute onion for 5 minutes, until soft.

4. Add spinach and cook until wilted.

5. Add egg and stir through, then allow to set for 10 minutes. In the last minute of cooking, flip one side of the omelette over the top of the other side.

6. Serve immediately, garnished with fresh spinach leaves.

HOMEMADE GRANOLA

INGREDIENTS

2 cups (180g, 6oz) whole rolled oats

1 cup (125g, 4oz) hazelnuts, whole and chopped

¼ cup (30g, 1oz) sunflower seeds

2 tbsps honey

2 tbsps coconut oil

½ tsp vanilla extract

Pinch of salt

METHOD

1. Preheat the oven to 150°C (300°F, Gas Mark 2).

2. Mix together all ingredients with hands until well combined and coated in oil.

3. Spread out mixture on a lined baking tray.

4. Bake for 10 minutes until golden.

5. Cool before serving. Store in an airtight container for up to 2 weeks.

SCRAMBLED TOFU ON TOAST

INGREDIENTS

Olive oil, for frying

¼ onion, finely diced

1 stalk celery, finely chopped

225g (8oz, ½ lb) silken tofu

1 tomato, finely diced

Handful of parsley, chopped

Handful of basil, torn

Rye bread, to serve

METHOD

1. Heat oil in a frying pan over a medium heat and saute onion and celery for 4 minutes, until celery is soft and onion translucent.

2. Add tofu to the frying pan and stir well to scramble.

3. Add tomato, parsley and basil and stir through.

4. Stir-fry tofu mix for 3 minutes until thoroughly heated through.

5. Serve with rye bread or toast, as desired.

ROASTED FENNEL CHERRY TOMATOES

INGREDIENTS

3 tbsps olive oil

Pinch of pepper

1 tbsp fennel seeds

1 clove garlic, minced

500g (1lb 2oz) cherry tomatoes, halved

METHOD

1. Preheat oven to 190°C (375°F, Gas Mark 5) and grease or line a baking tray.

2. Mix together oil, pepper and fennel seeds and garlic in a bowl.

3. Add tomatoes and toss to coat with oil.

4. Gently place tomatoes on baking tray.

5. Roast for 20 minutes, until soft and sizzling.

AVOCADO SCRAMBLED EGG WRAPS

INGREDIENTS

6 eggs

¼ cup (60ml, 2fl oz) milk

Salt and pepper, to taste

10g (¼ oz) butter

1 avocado, roughly chopped

4 flour tortilla wraps, warmed

Chives, chopped, to garnish

METHOD

1. Whisk eggs and milk in a bowl until well combined.

2. Season with salt and pepper.

3. Over a low heat, melt butter in a frying pan.

4. Add egg and gently stir for 4 minutes, until cooked. Remove from heat.

5. Add avocado and fold through scrambled egg.

6. To serve, evenly divide egg mix and spoon onto each tortilla. Wrap tortilla around egg mixture.

7. Sprinkle with chives to garnish.

SERVES 4 ★ PREP 5MIN (PLUS CHILLING) ★ COOK TIME 10MIN (PLUS STEEPING)

CHIA BERRY POTS WITH LAVENDER HONEY

INGREDIENTS

²/₃ cup (160ml, 5fl oz)
coconut cream

2 tbsps honey

Pinch of salt

½ vanilla bean,
split lengthwise
and scraped

½ cup (100g, 3oz)
chia seeds

2 cups (500ml, 1pt)
almond milk

Lavender honey

¼ cup (90g, 3oz)
mild honey

2 tsps culinary
lavender buds

2 cups (200g, 7oz)
fresh blueberries

2 kiwi fruit, sliced

Mint leaves,
to garnish

METHOD

1. Warm coconut cream in a saucepan on a low heat. Add honey, salt and vanilla seeds and pod and gently stir for 2 minutes until honey melts.

2. Remove from heat. Stir in chia seeds and almond milk. Set aside for 5 minutes to allow chia seeds to absorb.

3. Pour mixture into a jar, cover, and refrigerate for 3 hours.

4. Meanwhile, to make lavender honey, combine honey and lavender buds in a small saucepan over a low-medium heat until honey warms.

5. Remove from heat and allow honey to steep for 20 minutes, or more, to taste.

6. Reheat honey until it is liquid, then strain into a jar or container. Store at room temperature.

7. To serve, divide pudding evenly between four serving glasses.

8. Top each glass with blueberries and kiwi fruit. Drizzle with lavender honey, to taste. Garnish with mint leaves.

PROTEIN MUFFINS

INGREDIENTS

Muffins

1 banana, mashed

3 tbsps almond milk

6 egg whites

2½ cups (310g, 10oz) protein powder

3 tbsps almond flour

2 tbsps flax seed

¼ cup (40g, 1½ oz) apple sauce (unsweetened)

2 tbsps coconut oil, melted

1 tsp vanilla extract

1 tbsp cinnamon

2 tsps baking powder

1 tbsp sesame seeds

METHOD

1. Preheat oven to 180°C (355°F, Gas Mark 4) and grease a 12-hole muffin tin.

2. Mash banana and almond milk in a bowl until smooth.

3. Add egg whites, protein powder, flour, flaxseed, apple sauce, coconut oil, vanilla, cinnamon and baking powder to the bowl and mix thoroughly.

4. Spoon mixture into muffin tin. Sprinkle with sesame seeds.

5. Bake for 20 minutes, until muffins are cooked through, and serve warm.

ASPARAGUS FRITTATA

INGREDIENTS

½ cup (80g, 3oz) rice, cooked

½ cup (80g, 3oz) quinoa, cooked

6 egg whites

4 asparagus spears, trimmed and halved

Pepper and salt, to taste

METHOD

1. Set oven to 205°C (400°F, Gas Mark 6) and grease a baking dish.

2. Mix pre-cooked rice and quinoa together in a bowl.

3. Stir in the egg whites and mix until well combined, then add the asparagus. Season with salt and pepper.

4. Transfer mixture to a low-sided baking dish.

5. Bake for 15 minutes, until set and cooked through.

6. Remove from oven and slice into squares to serve.

OMELETTE WITH MUSHROOMS

INGREDIENTS

Olive oil, for frying

2 spring onions, chopped

2 cloves garlic, minced

250g (9oz) button mushrooms, sliced

Butter, for frying

4 large eggs

½ cup (125ml, 4fl oz) milk

1 tbsp dried mixed herbs

¼ cup (10g, ¼ oz) fresh chives, finely chopped (retain 1 tbsp for garnish)

METHOD

1. Heat olive oil in a frying pan over a medium heat. Add spring onions and garlic and saute for 3-5 minutes until soft.

2. Add the mushrooms and saute until soft. Remove from heat, cover with a plate or foil to keep warm and set aside.

3. Melt butter in a frying pan over medium-high heat.

4. Meanwhile, whisk eggs and milk together in a small bowl. Add dried herbs and fresh chives.

5. Pour half the egg mixture into the frying pan when butter has started to sizzle.

6. Cook until the egg is beginning to set on the surface.

7. Place half of the mushrooms on one side of omelette and cook until egg is firm and cooked through.

8. Slide omelette out of frying pan onto a serving plate and flip other side over to cover mushrooms.

9. Repeat with remaining ingredients for a second omelette.

10. Garnish with a sprinkle of chives and serve with toast.

COCONUT MANGO RICE PUDDING

INGREDIENTS

¾ cup (120g, 4oz) jasmine rice (or arborio rice)

1 x 400ml (14fl oz) can coconut milk

½ cup (125ml, 4fl oz) water

1 tbsp vanilla extract

Pinch of salt

½ cup (180g, 6oz) rice malt syrup

½ mango, diced

Mint leaves, to garnish

METHOD

1. Cook rice, coconut milk, water, vanilla extract, salt and rice malt syrup in a saucepan over a medium-low heat for 20 minutes.

2. Bring to the boil then reduce heat and simmer for 40 minutes, or until rice is cooked.

3. Allow rice to cool, then chill in refrigerator for 2 hours.

4. Spoon into serving glasses, mixing through mango cubes. Keep some mango aside for topping.

5. Serve topped with mango and garnished with mint leaves.

GRILLED SARDINES WITH LEMON

INGREDIENTS

3 garlic cloves, finely minced

¼ cup (60ml, 2fl oz) olive oil

1 lemon, juiced

2 tbsps parsley, chopped

½ tsp pepper

8-10 fresh sardines

Salt and pepper, to taste

Roasted cherry tomatoes and lemon wedges, to serve

METHOD

1. Rub the sardines with a paper towel to remove any scales. Pat dry.

2. Whisk garlic, oil, lemon juice, parsley and pepper together in a bowl.

3. Layer sardines flat in a shallow baking dish. Pour over lemon juice marinade. Cover and allow to marinate for 30 minutes.

4, Grill sardines on a medium-high heat for 2-3 minutes until cooked through, flipping over to lightly brown each side.

5. Season with salt and pepper. Serve with roasted tomatoes and lemon wedges.

RED QUINOA WITH APPLES

INGREDIENTS

1 cup (190g, 7oz) red quinoa, rinsed

2 cups (500ml, 1pt) water

¼ cup (30g, 1oz) flour

¼ cup (20g, ¾ oz) rolled oats

¼ tsp cinnamon

2 tbsps butter, melted

4 large apples, sliced

1 cup (250ml, 8fl oz) apple cider (or water)

Pinch of stevia powder

½ tsp vanilla extract

½ tsp cinnamon

2 cups (500ml, 1pt) plain Greek yoghurt

METHOD

1. Preheat oven to 180°C (355°F, Gas Mark 4).

2. Bring the quinoa, and enough water to cover, to the boil in a saucepan. Lower heat and simmer for 15 minutes until water has absorbed and the quinoa is tender.

3. Combine flour, oats, ¼ teaspoon cinnamon and butter in a bowl and mix well.

4. Spread oat and butter mix on baking tray and bake for 10 minutes, or until golden brown.

5. Meanwhile, bring apples, vinegar, stevia, vanilla and cinnamon to the boil. Lower the heat and simmer for 7 minutes until apples are soft and liquid is a syrup consistency.

6. To serve, place a layer of yoghurt in each serving glass, filling it a quarter full, followed by equal layers of oats, stewed apple and quinoa.

7. Top with a final layer of yoghurt and sprinkle with oats.

EGG BAKED IN AVOCADO

INGREDIENTS

2 ripe avocados, halved

4 eggs

Salt and pepper

1 tbsp parsley, chopped

METHOD

1. Preheat the oven to 220°C (430°F, Gas Mark 7).

2. Make a scoop in each avocado half, big enough to fit a poached egg.

3. Place avocado halves in a baking dish so that they fit together tightly.

4. Crack an egg into each scooped-out avocado.

5. Place in the oven and bake for 15 minutes, or until the egg whites have set.

6. Season with salt and cracked pepper and garnish with parsley.

COCO-CASHEW NUT BUTTER

INGREDIENTS

1½ cups (185g, 6oz) toasted cashews

¼ cup (20g, ¾ oz) coconut chips

1 tsp coconut oil

½ tsp salt

METHOD

1. In a food processor, blend cashews for 5 minutes, until smooth and creamy.

2. Add coconut chips, coconut oil and salt and continue to blend until combined.

3. Spread on bread or toast, to serve.

   Note: Can be kept in a sterilised jar at room temperature for 2 weeks, or in the fridge for up to 2 months.

WHOLE WHEAT BLACKBERRY PANCAKES

INGREDIENTS

2 cups (250g, 8oz) whole wheat flour

1 tbsp baking powder

½ tsp salt

¼ cup (20g, ¾ oz) quick oats

½ cup (80g, 3oz) blackberry puree

1 egg

1¼ cups (310ml, 10fl oz) milk

¼ cup (90g, 3oz) agave syrup

1 tsp vanilla extract

4 tbsps butter, melted

Butter, for cooking

Rice malt syrup, to serve

8 whole blackberries, to serve

METHOD

1. Mix flour, baking powder, salt, oats and blackberry puree in a bowl.

2. In a separate bowl, lightly whisk egg, milk, agave syrup, vanilla and melted butter.

3. In batches, pour the wet ingredients into the dry and stir until just combined (still a little lumpy).

4. Melt a small knob of butter in a small frying pan over a low-medium heat.

5. Pour a quarter of the batter into the frying pan and cook until bubbles form on the top of the pancake.

6. Flip onto the other side and continue cooking until golden brown.

7. Serve with a drizzle of rice malt syrup and garnish with whole berries to serve.

BLUEBERRY YOGHURT POT

INGREDIENTS

½ cup (50g, 2oz)
blueberries

½ cup (125ml, 4fl oz)
plain yoghurt

½ cup (125ml, 4fl oz) low
sugar berry yoghurt

⅓ cup (10g, ¼ oz) honey-
puffed wheat

METHOD

1. Divide plain yoghurt into two even portions and spoon each into a
    serving glass.

2. Divide berries into two even portions and spoon into serving glasses
    on top of yoghurt.

3. Top with the berry yoghurt, evenly divided between each serving
    glass.

4. Top each glass with the puffed wheat cereal.

OVERNIGHT OATMEAL

INGREDIENTS

1 ripe banana, mashed

1 cup (90g, 3oz) rolled oats

2 tsps chia seeds

¼ cup (30g, 1oz) toasted walnuts, chopped

1 cup (250ml, 8fl oz) almond milk, plus extra to serve

Honey or rice malt syrup (optional)

Extra banana slices and walnuts, to garnish

METHOD

1. Place banana, oats, chia seeds and walnuts in a container with a tight-fitting lid.

2. Stir in almond milk and sweetener of choice, if using, and stir.

3. Place lid on tightly and vigorously shake to combine.

4. Refrigerate overnight, or for 6 hours minimum.

5. To serve, add a splash of almond milk to thin out mixture if needed and top with banana slices and walnuts.

6. Top with a drizzle of honey or rice malt syrup, if desired.

FLORENTINE EGGS

INGREDIENTS

2 tsps butter

2 large bunches spinach,
leaves picked

Pinch of nutmeg

8 eggs

Salt and pepper

METHOD

1. Preheat oven to 200°C (390°F, Gas Mark 6). Grease four ramekins with butter.

2. Bring a large saucepan of water to the boil. Add spinach and cook for 30 seconds until wilted.

3. Transfer spinach to the food food processer. Season with nutmeg, salt, and pepper, and blend until pureed.

4. Divide spinach evenly and spoon into the ramekins, making a hollow in the centre of the spinach.

5. Into each hollow, break two eggs.

6. Bake for 10 minutes, until egg white has set but yolk is still runny.

7. Season with salt and pepper to serve.

QUINOA PORRIDGE BOWL

INGREDIENTS

1¼ cups (310ml, 10fl oz) milk

¾ cup (150g, 5oz) white quinoa seeds, rinsed well

1 tbsp chia seeds

½ tsp maple syrup

Pinch of ground cinnamon

Pinch of salt

½ cup (50g, 2oz) fresh blueberries

To serve

1 tbsp almond flakes

Handful of blueberries

1 tbsp cooked quinoa

¼ ground cinnamon

METHOD

1. Bring the milk to the boil in a small saucepan over a medium heat.

2. Add quinoa and chia seeds. Lower heat and simmer, covered, for 15 minutes.

3. Add the maple syrup, cinnamon and salt and simmer for 10 minutes, until nearly all milk absorbed.

4. Gently stir through blueberries and cook for 1 minute.

5. To serve, spoon porridge into serving bowls and top with almond flakes, blueberries, quinoa and cinnamon.

CINNAMON RICE PORRIDGE

INGREDIENTS

½ cup (80g, 3oz) rice

1 cup (250ml, 8fl oz) water

1 cinnamon quill

2 cups (500ml, 1pt) milk

1 tsp of cinnamon, to serve

1 tsp ground cinnamon, to garnish

METHOD

1. Place rice, water and cinnamon quill in a saucepan over medium-high heat and bring to the boil. Reduce heat to a simmer for 5 minutes, until water absorbed.

2. Add the milk and stir gently.

3. Simmer for 20 minutes over a low-medium heat until the rice is cooked and milk absorbed.

4. Serve on its own, or with milk, if desired, and top with a sprinkle of cinnamon.

POACHED EGG WITH SPINACH

INGREDIENTS

4 eggs

2 tbsps white vinegar

1 tbsp olive oil

250g (9oz) baby spinach leaves

1 garlic clove

100g (3½ oz) blue cheese (such as gorgonzola)

Salt and pepper

METHOD

1. Fill a large frying pan three quarters full with water and bring to a simmer.

2. Crack egg into a small bowl and gently slip it into the water. Repeat with each egg.

3. Add vinegar to the water. Turn off heat and cover the frying pan. Allow eggs to cook for 4 minutes, until whites have set.

4. While eggs are cooking, heat oil in a frying pan. Add spinach and garlic clove. Wilt spinach for 2 minutes. Discard garlic.

5. Remove from heat and divide spinach between serving plates.

6. Gently lift the poached eggs out of the water pan with a slotted spoon, drain off excess water and place on top of the bed of spinach.

7. Crumble blue cheese over the top and season with salt and pepper to serve.

SOUPS
AND
SALADS

Parsley andthree bean salad 44

Rosemary and lemon dressing 45

Bean and barley salad bowl 46

Red lentil soup 48

Spring rice salad 49

Orange, pistachio and beetroot salad 50

Simple pea soup 52

Miso with udon noodles 53

Chicken noodle miso bowl 54

Classic pumpkin soup 56

Walnut and bean salad 57

Sesame miso chicken 58

Warm salad of green beans and bacon 60

Homemade mayonnaise 61

Nourishing quinoa and feta salad 62

Broad bean salad 64

Bone broth 65

Zesty warm chicken salad 66

Warm chicken salad 68

Easy seafood chowder 69

Glazed ginger prawns 70

Sweet kale salad 72

Green godess soup 73

Spicy sausage, lentil and tomato soup 74

Roast beetroot salad with homemade dukkah 76

Potato salad with crispy bacon 77

PARSLEY AND THREE BEAN SALAD

INGREDIENTS

1 x 400g (14oz) can kidney beans, drained and rinsed

1 x 400g (14oz) can cannellini beans, drained and rinsed

1 x 400g (14oz) can chickpeas, drained and rinsed

200g corn kernels, cooked

1 red onion, finely chopped

Rosemary and lemon dressing (see recipe p75)

Salt and pepper

1 bunch flat leaf parsley, leaves picked and chopped

METHOD

1. Mix all beans, corn and onion together in a serving bowl.

2. Toss with rosemary and lemon salad dressing and season salad to taste with salt and pepper.

3. Top with flat-leaf parsley to serve.

    Note: Different bean varieties can be substituted, if desired.

SERVES 4 ★ PREP 5MIN

ROSEMARY AND LEMON DRESSING

INGREDIENTS

3 tbsps fresh lemon juice

½ tsp Dijon mustard

¾ cup (185ml, 6fl oz) olive oil

1 clove garlic, minced

2 tsps rosemary, finely chopped

Salt and pepper, to taste

METHOD

1. Mix all ingredients in a jar or container with a tight fitting lid.

2. Place lid on tightly and shake container vigorously until all ingredients are throroughly combined.

3. Shake again well just before using.

SERVES 4 ★ PREP 10MIN ★ COOK TIME 45MIN

BEAN AND BARLEY SALAD BOWL

INGREDIENTS

1½ cup (275g, 9oz) barley

3 cups (750ml, 24fl oz) water

½ tsp salt

1 tbsp olive oil

1 clove garlic, slivered

150g (5oz) mushrooms, sliced

1 large bunch of spinach, leaves torn

2 lemons, zested

1 tbsp dill, chopped

1 x 400g (14oz) can white beans, drained and rinsed

Salt and pepper, to taste

METHOD

1. Place the barley, water and salt in a large saucepan over medium-high heat. Bring to the boil, then reduce heat to low and cover the pan. Simmer for 45 minutes, or until liquid absorbed. Drain and set aside.

2. While barley cooks, heat oil in a large frying pan over a medium heat.

3. Add garlic and cook for 1 minute.

4. Add mushrooms and cook for 5 minutes, until tender.

5. Add spinach and a pinch of salt and cook for 1-2 minutes until spinach wilts.

6. Remove from heat and place into a large bowl. Add lemon zest, dill and white beans and stir to combine.

7. Stir in the barley and mix ingredients together until just combined.

8. Serve warm. Season with salt and pepper, to taste.

RED LENTIL SOUP

INGREDIENTS

1 tbsp olive oil

1 onion, diced

1 carrot, diced

2 stalks celery, diced

½ red capsicum,
de-seeded and diced

¼ tsp salt

1 cup (185g, 6oz) red
lentils

4 cups (1L, 2pt) vegetable
stock (or water)

1 bay leaf

2 tbsps lemon juice

METHOD

1. Heat oil in a large saucepan over a medium heat.

2. Add onion, carrot, celery, capsicum and salt and stir to combine. Reduce heat to low. Cover with lid and sweat vegetables for 5 minutes, until onion is soft and translucent.

3. Add lentils, stock and bay leaf.

4. Increase heat and bring to the boil. Lower heat and simmer for 20 minutes, until lentils are soft and breaking apart.

5. Remove from heat and stir in lemon juice.

6. Discard bay leaf and season with salt, to taste, before serving.

SPRING RICE SALAD

INGREDIENTS

1 tbsp olive oil

3 cups (465g, 12oz) basmati rice

6 cups (1.5L, 50fl oz) water

300g (10oz) green beans, trimmed

2 zucchinis, (1 yellow, 1 green), cut in half lengthwise, then sliced into half moons

1 cup (170g, 6oz) peas (fresh or frozen)

Handful of fresh parsley leaves, to garnish

Dressing

²/₃ cup (160ml, 5fl oz) olive oil

¹/₃ cup (80ml, 3fl oz) white wine vinegar

Pinch of salt and pepper

METHOD

1. Heat oil in a saucecepan over a medium heat. Add rice and cook for 1 minute, stirring.

2. Add water to the saucepan and bring to the boil. Reduce heat and simmer for 12 minutes until water is fully absorbed. Set aside to cool.

3. Bring a saucepan of water to the boil over medium heat. Steam the beans, zucchini and peas for 1-2 minutes.

4. Drain and refresh in very cold water. Set aside.

5. Mix dressing by combining oil, vinegar, salt and pepper in a jar or container with a tight fitting lid. Tighten lid. Shake vigorously until well combined.

6. Toss vegetables through rice.

7. Add dressing before serving. Garnish with parsley.

SERVES 2 ★ PREP 15MIN ★ COOK TIME 35MIN

ORANGE, PISTACHIO AND BEETROOT SALAD

INGREDIENTS

1½ cups (375ml, 13fl oz) vegetable stock

1 tsp salt

1 cup (190g, 7oz) quinoa

3 beetroots, trimmed

1 tbsp olive oil and 1 tbsp red wine vinegar (mixed)

1 cup (30g, 1oz) coriander, finely chopped

1 cup (30g, 1oz) flat-leaf parsley, finely chopped

1 cup (100g, 3½ oz) pomegranate seeds

1 cup (125g, 4oz) pistachios, roughly chopped

1 orange, peeled and sliced

METHOD

1. Place stock in a saucepan and bring stock to a boil over a medium heat. Add salt and quinoa. Lower heat and simmer for 15 minutes.

2. Remove from heat and leave quinoa to soak in the pan, covered, for 15 minutes, until liquid has absorbed. Fluff with a fork. Allow to cool.

3. Meanwhile, bring a medium saucepan of salted water to a boil and add the beetroots. Simmer over medium heat for 20 minutes.

4. Drain and rinse under cool water. Remove skins and dice.

5. Toss beetroots with oil and vinegar mixture in a large bowl. Add quinoa, coriander and parsley and toss to combine thoroughly.

6. Add most of the pomegranate seeds and pistachios, reserving some for garnishing.

7. Transfer to serving bowls and arrange orange slices on top.

8. Top with a remaining pomegranate and pistachios, to serve.

SIMPLE PEA SOUP

INGREDIENTS

2 tbsps coconut oil

1 onion, chopped

2 cups (500ml, 1pt) vegetable stock

2 cups (500ml, 1pt) water

500g (1lb 2oz) frozen peas

1 cup (45g, 1½ oz) fresh mint, chopped, leaving aside a few leaves for garnish

1 cup (45g, 1½ oz) parsley, chopped

2 tsps salt

½ tsp pepper

METHOD

1. Heat the coconut oil in a saucepan over a medium heat. Add onion and cook, stirring, for 5 minutes, until soft.

2. Increase the heat to high. Add the stock and water, and bring to a boil.

3. Add peas and cook at a rolling boil for 3 minutes, until peas are tender.

4. Remove from heat. Add mint and parsley. Season with salt and pepper.

5. Blend in the pan using an immersion blender or in batches in a food processor until smooth and creamy.

MISO WITH UDON NOODLES

INGREDIENTS

10g (1oz) dried wakame
seaweed

1 tsp yellow or red miso

Sriracha or other Asian
hot sauce, to taste
(optional)

1 tsp ponzu sauce
(or soy sauce)

2 cups (500ml, 1pt) water

2 tsps soy sauce

2 thin slices ginger

1 clove garlic, finely sliced

1 carrot, thinly sliced

2 asparagus spears,
halved

3 large shitake
mushrooms, thickly
sliced

100g (3½ oz) firm tofu,
cubed

85g (3oz) udon noodles,
cooked

METHOD

1. Cover wakame with warm water and let stand 15 minutes.
    Drain and set aside.

2. Whisk together the miso and ½ cup (125ml, 4fl oz) water. Add
    Sriracha and ponzu sauce.

3. Mix water with soy sauce, ginger and garlic and bring to the boil
    in a saucepan.

4. Reduce heat and simmer for 10 minutes.

5. Add carrot, asparagus, shitake mushrooms and tofu, and simmer
    for 4-5 minutes, until vegetables are soft.

6. Gently stir in the miso mix.

7. Serve in large soup bowls.

CHICKEN NOODLE MISO BOWL

INGREDIENTS

3 garlic cloves, minced

Medium piece ginger, minced

1 tbsp soy sauce

4 cups (1L, 2pt)

chicken stock

225g (8oz, ½ lb)

soba noodles

2 tbsps miso paste

1 tsp ponzu sauce

2 chicken breasts, thinly sliced

2 tsps sesame oil

2 tbsps lime juice

Red chilli, finely sliced, to garnish

Green salad, to serve

METHOD

1. Heat the oil in a large saucepan over medium heat. Add the garlic and ginger, and cook, stirring, for 5 minutes until softened.

2. Add the stock, cover and bring to a boil. Stir in miso paste, ponzu and lime juice and noodles and cook for 2-3 minutes. Remove from heat, cover and set aside.

3. Heat the sesame oil in a large frying pan over medium-high heat. Add the chicken and stir-fry for 5-6 minutes until golden and cooked through. Place the chicken in the pan with the soup.

4. When ready to serve, divide the soup between large bowls and garnish with salad and fresh chilli.

CLASSIC PUMPKIN SOUP

INGREDIENTS

3 cups (750ml, 24fl oz)
chicken or vegetable
stock

1 kg (2lb) pumpkin,
cut into large chunks

2 onions, sliced

2 cloves garlic, minced

1 cup (250ml, 8fl oz) milk

Salt and pepper, to
season

Sour cream, to serve

METHOD

1. Bring a large saucepan of stock to the boil over a medium-high heat.

2. Add pumpkin, onion and garlic. Reduce heat and simmer for
    25-30 minutes, until pumpkin is soft.

3. Remove from heat and use an immersion blender to puree
    ingredients into a smooth and creamy soup. (You can also process in
    batches using a stand-up blender).

4. Return soup to the pan (if using a stand-up blender)
    and return pan to the heat. Add milk and season with salt
    and pepper. Cook for 2-3 minutes until warmed through.

5. Add a spoonful of sour cream to each bowl before serving.

WALNUT AND BEAN SALAD

INGREDIENTS

¼ cup (30g, 1oz) walnuts, chopped

450g (1lb) green beans, trimmed

Rosemary and lemon dressing (see recipe p75)

METHOD

1. Heat a small frying pan over a medium heat. Add walnuts and dry fry for 5 minutes until aromatic. Set aside.

2. Meanwhile, bring a saucepan of salted water to the boil.

3. Add beans and reduce heat to a simmer. Cook for 4 minutes until beans are tender, but not too soft.

4. Drain well.

5. To serve, place beans in a large serving bowl and toss through walnuts and lemon dressing, to taste.

SESAME MISO CHICKEN

INGREDIENTS

Marinade

⅓ cup (80ml, 3fl oz) miso paste

2 tsps sesame oil

⅓ cup (80ml, 3fl oz) mirin

3 chicken breasts, trimmed

200g (7oz) snow peas

2 bunches baby spinach, leaves picked

1 lemon

Black sesame seeds, to garnish

Sesame oil, to serve (optional)

METHOD

1. Combine marinade ingredients in a bowl and mix.

2. Toss chicken through marinade until well coated. Cover and transfer to the refrigerator for 30 minutes.

3. When ready to cook, preheat grill to a medium heat.

4. Grill chicken for 7-8 minutes on each side until cooked through.

5. Remove from heat and cut into pieces. Cover and keep warm.

6. Bring a saucepan of salted water to the boil and blanch snowpeas until al dente. Dip into chilled water and drain.

7. Repeat with baby spinach leaves, blanching quickly to wilt leaves.

8. Combine spinach and snow peas on serving plates and squeeze lemon over greens, to taste.

9. Arrange chicken on top of greens. Top with black sesame seeds and a splash of sesame oil, if desired.

SERVES 6 ★ PREP 10MIN ★ COOK TIME 30MIN

WARM SALAD OF GREEN BEANS AND BACON

INGREDIENTS

1.5kg (3lb 5oz) green beans, trimmed

500g (1lb 2oz) bacon, roughly chopped

1 onion, chopped

1 orange or yellow capsicum, diced

3 cloves garlic, minced

1 tsp chilli flakes (optional)

½ cup (60g, 2oz) toasted pecans, chopped

Juice of ½ lemon

Salt and pepper

Black and white sesame seeds, to serve

METHOD

1. Steam beans until tender then remove from heat. Refresh in a ice water. Drain and set aside.

2. Saute bacon in a large frying pan for 5 minutes, until crisp. Remove from heat and set aside.

3. Saute onions and capsicum in the same frying pan on a medium heat for 5 minutes until soft.

4. Add garlic and chilli, if using, and saute for 1 minute.

5. Add green beans and pecans and saute for 5 minutes.

6. Return bacon to the frying pan and toss with lemon juice.

7. Season with salt and pepper.

8. Serve with sesame seeds sprinkled over the top.

SERVES 4 ★ PREP 15MIN

HOMEMADE MAYONNAISE

INGREDIENTS

1 large egg yolk

1½ tsps fresh lemon juice

1 tsp white wine vinegar

¼ tsp Dijon mustard

½ tsp salt

¾ cup (185ml, 6fl oz)
olive oil

METHOD

1. Whisk together the egg yolk, lemon juice, vinegar, mustard
    and salt until blended and bright yellow.

2. Gradually add a quarter of the olive oil and whisk by hand for
    4 minutes.

3. Whisk in remaining oil gradually, untiled mayonnaise thickens
    to the desired consistency. This may take 10 minutes.

4. Cover and refrigerate. Keep chilled before serving.

NOURISHING QUINOA AND FETA SALAD

INGREDIENTS

1 large eggplant, diced

4 tbsps olive oil, divided

Salt and pepper, to season

2 cloves garlic, minced

½ cup (15g, ½ oz) fresh spinach

4 cups (750g, 1½ lb) cooked quinoa

1 cup (125g, 4oz) feta cheese, crumbled

METHOD

1. Preheat oven to 215°C (420°F, Gas Mark 7). Grease a baking tray.

2. Toss eggplant with 3 tablespoons of olive oil until well coated. Season with salt and pepper.

3. Place on baking tray and roast for 25 minutes, until eggplant is tender. Remove and transfer to a mixing bowl.

4. Meanwhile, heat 1 tablespoon of oil in a frying pan over a medium heat.

5. Saute half of the minced garlic and all of the spinach leaves for 3 minutes, until garlic is soft and spinach has wilted. Remove from heat

6. Add quinoa and remaining garlic and toss through until well combined.

7. Gently mix through spinach leaves.

8. Serve with feta crumbled on top.

BROAD BEAN SALAD

INGREDIENTS

300g (10oz) fresh broad beans

1 tbsp olive oil

3 bacon rashers, sliced

1 cup (170g, 6oz) fresh peas

Salt and pepper, to season

½ red onion, sliced

1 punnet cherry tomatoes, halved

Olive oil, extra, to serve

METHOD

1. Cover broad beans with boiling water in a bowl and set aside, covered, for 5 minutes.

2. Drain and allow to cool slightly. Peel beans.

3. In a frying pan over a high heat, fry bacon in olive oil for 5 minutes, until crispy.

4. Add beans and peas and cook for 5 minutes until beans and peas are heated through and tender. Season with salt and pepper.

5. Place warm beans and peas in a salad bowl. Toss through cherry tomatoes and red onion. Drizzle with extra olive oil.

BONE BROTH

INGREDIENTS

1kg (2lb) meat bones (reserved from a roast or bought from a butcher)

2 tbsps apple cider vinegar

1 onion, roughly chopped

2 carrots, roughly chopped

2 stalks celery, roughly chopped

1 tbsp salt

1 tsp pepper

2 garlic cloves, chopped

1 bunch parsley, chopped

METHOD

1. Place bones in an oven preheated to 180°C (355°F, Gas Mark 4) and roast for 30 minutes.

2. Transfer bones to a large stock pot or saucepan and fill with water. Add vinegar. Steep for 30 minutes.

3. Add the onion, carrots and celery. Season with salt and pepper.

4. Over a medium-high heat, bring the broth to a rolling boil. Reduce heat to a simmer for 2 hours.

5. Remove impurities that float to the surface and discard.

6. Add garlic and parsley in last 30 minutes.

7. Remove from heat. Allow broth to cool before straining.

8. If not using immediately, store in fridge for up to 5 days, or freeze.

SERVES 2 ★ PREP 10MIN ★ COOK TIME 45MIN

ZESTY WARM CHICKEN SALAD

INGREDIENTS

3 tbsps olive oil

2 tsps fresh thyme

1 tsp salt

2 tsps pepper

2 beetroots, diced

1 red onion, very finely sliced

2 chicken breasts

1 bunch kale, leaves picked

1 orange, peeled and cut into pieces

3 tbsps balsamic vinegar

3 tbsps goat's cheese, crumbled

Handful pepitas, sunflower seeds and flaxseed, to serve

METHOD

1. Preheat oven to 205°C (400°F, Gas Mark 6).

2. Combine 1 tablespoon of olive oil with thyme, salt and pepper in a bowl.

3. Add beetroots and onion to the seasoned oil, and toss until well coated. Place on a baking tray.

4. Place beetroots and onion in the oven and roast for 45 minutes, until caramelised and soft.

5. Rub chicken with 1 tablespoon of olive oil and place in a baking dish. Place in the oven and cook for 20 minutes, until golden and cooked through.

6. Remove chicken from oven. When cooled slightly, slice into bite-sized chunks. Cover to keep warm.

7. Meanwhile, rub remaining olive oil onto kale leaves. Massage for 3 minutes until leaves are soft and fully coated. Set aside for 30 minutes.

8. When beetroot is cooked place in a bowl with chicken and orange. Pour over the balsamic vinegar and toss to combine. Season with salt and pepper.

9. Serve warm on a bed of kale. Top with goat's cheese and seeds.

SERVES 4 ★ PREP 10MIN (PLUS MARINATING) ★ COOK TIME 5MIN

WARM CHICKEN SALAD

INGREDIENTS

220g (8oz) pearl barley

1 lemon, zested

2 tbsps lemon juice, divided

4 tbsps olive oil, divided

¼ tsp fennel seeds, crushed

1 garlic clove, minced

Salt and pepper

2 chicken breasts, cut into strips

1 bunch tatsoi (or other Asian green), leaves and stalks

2 spring onions, sliced diagonally

1 tbsp honey

2 tbsps wholegrain mustard

1 tbsp vinegar

METHOD

1. Cook barley according to the instructions on the packet. Set aside, covered to keep warm.

2. Meanwhile, mix lemon zest, 1 tablespoon of lemon juice, 1 tablespoon of olive oil, fennel seeds and garlic together in a small bowl. Season with salt and pepper. Toss chicken pieces through the mixture and leave to marinate for 20 minutes.

3. Heat 1 tablespoon of olive oil in a frying pan over a medium heat and saute chicken for 8 minutes, until cooked through. Remove from pan and cover to keep warm.

4. Add 1 tablespoon olive oil to frying pan and saute tatsoi and spring onion for 3 minutes, until tatsoi wilts.

5. Mix honey, mustard, vinegar, remaining oil and 1 tablespoon of lemon juice. Toss the pearl barley, chicken, vegetables and dressing together. Serve warm.

EASY SEAFOOD CHOWDER

INGREDIENTS

2 tbsps butter

1 onion, finely chopped

2 stalks celery, finely chopped

1 tsp thyme (fresh or dried)

1 bay leaf

Salt and pepper, to taste

2 large potatoes, peeled and diced

2 cups (500ml, 1pt) fish stock (or water)

⅓ cup (40g, 1½ oz) plain flour

3 cups (750ml, 24fl oz) milk

1 skinless fish fillet, chopped

300g (10oz) cooked mixed seafood

2 tbsps lemon juice, freshly squeezed

METHOD

1. Melt butter in a large saucepan over a medium heat. Add the onion, celery, thyme and bay leaf and fry for 5 minutes until onions soften and begin to brown.

2. Season with salt and pepper. Add potatoes and saute for a further 2 minutes.

3. Add stock and increase heat to bring to the boil. Cover pot. Reduce heat to medium and simmer for 5 minutes until potatoes are tender.

4. Mix flour and milk together, then add to saucepan. Add fish and seafood and simmer for 5 minutes until seafood is cooked and soup is creamy.

5. Add lemon juice. Season with salt and pepper.

6. Discard bay leaf. Serve immediately.

GLAZED GINGER PRAWNS

INGREDIENTS

¼ cup (60ml, 2fl oz) soy sauce

¼ cup (90g, 3oz) honey

1 tbsp rice wine vinegar

Small piece of ginger, minced

1 garlic clove, minced

½ tsp pepper

500g (1lb 2oz) prawns (peeled and deveined)

Sesame oil, to cook

2 tsps cornflour

Mixed green salad – salad leaves, radishes, cherry tomatoes

METHOD

1. Preheat oven to 180°C (355°F, Gas Mark 4) and line a baking tray.

2. Combine soy sauce, honey, vinegar, ginger, garlic and pepper in a small bowl and whisk until well combined.

3. Pour marinade over prawns, cover with plastic wrap and allow to marinate in the fridge for 30 minutes.

4. Remove prawns from marinade and place on baking tray. Drizzle with sesame oil.

5. Transfer to the oven and bake for 5 minutes, until cooked.

6. Meanwhile, bring remaining marinade to a boil in a small saucepan, add cornflour and whisk at a simmer until smooth.

7. Prepare a mixed green salad.

8. Arrange prawns on salad and dress with warm marinade.

SWEET KALE SALAD

INGREDIENTS

1 sweet potato, unpeeled, cut into bite-sized pieces

1 tbsp cayenne pepper

3 tbsps olive oil

Dressing

3 tbsps lemon juice

¼ cup (60ml, 2fl oz) olive oil

2 tbsps Dijon mustard

1 garlic clove, minced

½ tsp salt

½ tsp pepper

Salad

I bunch kale leaves, ribs removed, leaves torn

1 avocado, sliced

1 x 250g (9oz) punnet mixed cherry tomatoes, halved

2 tbsps pepitas

1 tbsp nutritional yeast (or flax seed), to serve

METHOD

1. Preheat the oven to 200°C (400°F, Gas Mark 6), and line a baking tray.

2. Place the sweet potato, olive oil, salt and cayenne pepper in a mixing bowl and toss to coat. Turn out onto baking tray and spread into an even layer. Transfer to the oven to roast for 20 minutes, until soft and slightly caramelised.

3. Place lemon juice, oil, mustard, garlic, salt and pepper in a container with a tight fitting lid. Shake vigorously until dressing is well combined.

4. Place kale, avocado, cherry tomatoes and pepitas in a serving dish.

5. Pour over the dressing and toss until well coated.

6. Sprinkle with nutritional yeast, serve.

GREEN GODDESS SOUP

INGREDIENTS

1 tbsp olive oil

1 onion, chopped

2 carrots, finely diced

300g (10oz) green beans, chopped

1 potato, finely diced

½ leek, sliced

1 stalk celery, chopped

1 garlic clove, finely chopped

1 bay leaf

½ cup (20g, ¾ oz) dill, finely chopped (reserve some for ganish)

6 cups (1.5L, 50fl oz) vegetable stock

Salt and pepper, to season

300g (10oz) peas (fresh or frozen)

1 garlic clove, grated, to garnish (optional)

METHOD

1. Heat the oil in large, deep frying pan or large saucepan. Add onion, carrot, beans, potato, leek and celery and saute for 3-4 minutes until softened.

2. Add garlic and saute for 1 minute.

3. Add the bay leaf, dill and vegetable stock.

4. Season with salt and pepper.

5. Bring to a boil and then reduce to a simmer. Cook for 15 minutes.

6. Add peas. Bring back to the boil then reduce to a simmer for 2 minutes. Remove from heat.

7. Season to taste. Garnish with reserved dill and raw garlic, if desired.

SPICY SAUSAGE, LENTIL AND TOMATO SOUP

INGREDIENTS

1 onion, chopped

2 celery stalks, finely diced

Olive oil, for frying

2 cloves garlic, minced

½ tsp chilli flakes

½ tsp dried thyme

1 tsp dried oregano

1 tsp ground fennel seed

4 spicy sausages, chopped

6 cups (1.5L, 50fl oz) chicken stock

2 x 400g (14oz) cans diced tomatoes

1½ cups (275g, 9oz) brown lentils

1 bay leaf

Salt and pepper, to season

Fresh parsley, to garnish

METHOD

1. Saute onion and celery in 2 tablespoons of oil in a frying pan for 5 minutes over a medium heat until onion begins to brown.

2. Add garlic and saute for 1 minute.

3. Add chilli flakes, dried thyme, dried oregano, and ground fennel seed and saute for 1 minute.

4. Transfer mixture into a large saucepan.

5. Add remaining olive oil to the frying pan. Add sausages and fry, turning, for 1-2 minutes, until browned on all sides.

6. Transfer sausage to saucepan with onions. Add chicken stock, tomatoes, lentils and bay leaf.

7. Heat to boiling point, then reduce heat to a simmer and cook for 1 hour, until lentils are soft.

8. Once lentils have softened, remove a third of the mixture and blend in a food processor until smooth.

9. Return pureed soup back to saucepan and stir. Simmer for 20 minutes until thickened as desired.

10. Season with salt and pepper and serve garnished with parsley.

ROAST BEETROOT SALAD WITH HOMEMADE DUKKAH

INGREDIENTS

2 bunches baby beetroots, diced

Olive oil, for roasting

Dressing

¼ cup (60ml, 2fl oz) olive oil

1½ tbsps red wine vinegar

1 tsp honey

1 tsp Dijon mustard

Dukkah

½ cup (80g, 3oz) sesame seeds

2 tbsps coriander seeds

2 tbsps cumin seeds

1 cup (125g, 4oz) hazelnuts

1 tsp flaked sea salt

2 tsps freshly ground black pepper

Salad

2 bunches rocket, leaves picked

200g (7oz) soft blue cheese, coarsely crumbled

METHOD

1. Preheat oven to 180°C (355°F, Gas Mark 4). Place beetroot on a baking tray and toss with olive oil. Bake for 30 minutes, until tender. Set aside.

2. Meanwhile, prepare the dressing by combining oil, vinegar, honey and mustard in a jar or container with a tight fitting lid. Tighten lid and shake vigorously until ingredients are well combined. Season to taste with salt and pepper.

3. Dry roast the sesame, coriander and cumin seeds in a frying pan until aromatic and slightly golden. Add hazelnuts and roast until golden and aromatic.

4. Using a mortar and pestle, or a grinder, grind the ingredients for the dukkah together to a coarse powder.

5. Arrange rocket leaves with the beetroot and blue cheese and scatter with dukkah to serve.

POTATO SALAD WITH CRISPY BACON

INGREDIENTS

8 potatoes, peeled

8 bacon rashers, sliced

¼ cup (60ml, 2fl oz) white vinegar

2 tbsps water

1 tsp salt

½ tsp pepper

1 tsp celery seed (or 1 stalk celery, finely sliced)

1 onion, sliced

Flat leaf parsley, to garnish

METHOD

1. Boil potatoes in salted water for 20 minutes, until tender. Drain and set aside until cool, then cut into small wedges.

2. Fry bacon in a large frying pan for 5 minutes, until crispy. Remove bacon from pan and set aside, retaining drippings.

3. Mix vinegar, water, salt, pepper and celery seed together in a small bowl. Add to frying pan with bacon drippings. Heat for 2 minutes until mixture thickens.

4. Add celery mix to potatoes and toss until well-coated. Season with salt and pepper.

5. Add onion to the same frying pan and fry, stirring, for 8-10 minutes until soft and caramelised.

6. Serve potatoes warm. Top with bacon and onion and garnish with parsley.

SNACKS AND LIGHT LUNCHES

Smoked turkey and vegetable tarts	80
Zucchini fritters	82
The business burgers	83
Cheesy zucchini bread	84
Gluten-free pizza	86
Kale chips	87
Sun-dried tomato tart	88
Power nutbread	90
Peanut butter cookies	91
Rye galette with ricotta and mushrooms	92
Wholesome nut and seed loaf	94
Broccoli and corn quesadilla	95
Beef soba noodles	96
Tahini dressing	98
Asparagus tart	99
Flax and sesame seed crackers	100
Green pea fritters	102
Black bean dip	103
Steamed mussels in white wine sauce	104
Feta and spinach pancakes	106
Savoury millet porridge	107
Quinoa fritters with poached eggs	108
Chicken frittata	110
Broad bean patties	112
Avocado hummus	113
Date, nut and chocolate bars	114
Cashew oat bars	116
Pumpkin oat cookies	117
Chocolate and beetroot muffins	118
Sesame date bliss balls	120
Lemon and lime cake	121
Peanut butter bars	122

SMOKED TURKEY AND VEGETABLE TARTS

INGREDIENTS

Pastry

2 cups (250g, 8oz) wholemeal flour

10 tbsps unsalted butter, chilled, diced

Pinch of salt

6 tbsps very cold water

Filling

2 spring onions, sliced thinly

1 clove garlic, chopped

2 tbsps olive oil

1 zucchini, finely diced

300g (10oz) button mushrooms, sliced thinly

Salt and pepper

100g (3½ oz) smoked turkey, cut into pieces

3 eggs

1 cup (250ml, 8fl oz) milk

4 cherry tomatoes

METHOD

1. Preheat oven to 180°C (355°F, Gas Mark 4) and grease four small tart tins.

2. Combine flour, butter and a pinch of salt and pulse in a food processor until the mixture resembles coarse breadcrumbs.

3. Mix in cold water until a firm, not too sticky, dough forms.

4. Cover dough in plastic wrap and refrigerate for 1 hour.

5. Meanwhile, saute spring onions and garlic in oil for 5 minutes until tender.

6. Add zucchini and mushrooms and saute for 3 minutes, until golden brown. Season with salt and pepper and remove from heat. Add turkey to the pan and stir to combine.

7. Whisk together eggs and milk and set aside.

8. Roll pastry and press into the base and around edges of the tart tins. Remove any excess with a knife.

9. Spoon the mushroom and turkey mixture into the tart tins. Pour egg mixture on top and place a cherry tomato in the centre.

10. Bake for 35 minutes, until golden brown and cooked through.

ZUCCHINI FRITTERS

INGREDIENTS

2 zucchinis, grated

1 tsp salt

2 eggs, beaten

2 spring onions, finely chopped

2 tbsps fresh dill, finely chopped

100g (3½ oz) feta cheese, crumbled

1 garlic clove, minced

¼ tsp pepper

¼ cup (30g, 1oz) plain flour

½ tsp baking powder

Olive oil, for frying

Salad greens, to serve

Sprig of dill, to garnish

METHOD

1. Toss zucchini with salt and place in a strainer for 10 minutes. Squeeze out excess liquid. Set aside.

2. Combine eggs with zucchini, spring onions, dill, feta, garlic and pepper in a large mixing bowl.

3. Stir in flour and baking powder and mix until thoroughly combined.

4. Heat olive oil in a large frying pan over a medium heat.

5. Spoon in 2 tablespoonfuls of batter and flatten with back of spoon.

6. Fry for 2 minutes then turn over and fry for a further 2 minutes, until golden. Transfer to a plate lined with a paper towel to absorb grease.

7. Repeat with remaining batter.

8. Garnish with dill and serve with salad greens.

THE BUSINESS BURGERS

INGREDIENTS

1 x 400g (14oz) can black beans rinsed, drained

½ pumpkin, cooked and mashed

1 cup (155g, 4oz) millet, cooked

1 carrot, finely grated

¼ onion, finely grated

½ cup (80g, 3oz) fresh corn kernels

¼ cup (50g, 2oz) cornmeal

1 tsp smoked paprika

1 tsp oregano (fresh or dried)

½ tsp ground cumin

½ tsp ground tumeric

1 tsp tamari (or soy sauce)

Salt and pepper, to season

Olive oil, for frying

4 hamburger buns, to serve

Salad fillings of choice

METHOD

1. Mix black beans, pumpkin and millet together in a large mixing bowl until well combined.

2. Add carrot, onion and corn and stir to mix well.

3. Add cornmeal, paprika, oregano, cumin and tamari and mix until fully combined.

4. Season with salt and pepper.

5. Evenly divide mixture and form into 4 patties of equal size.

6. Heat oil in a frying pan over a medium-high heat and fry each pattie individually for 4 minutes on each side, until heated through and golden. Repeat with rest of mixture.

7. Serve on hamburger buns with salad fillings.

CHEESY ZUCCHINI BREAD

INGREDIENTS

2 cups (250g, 8oz)
plain flour

2 tsps baking powder

½ tsp bicarbonate
of soda

¼ tsp salt

¼ tsp pepper

Pinch of cayenne pepper

2 tbsps spring onions,
finely chopped

1 cup (125g, 4oz)
cheddar cheese, grated

2 eggs

½ cup (125ml, 4fl oz)
milk

¼ cup (60ml, 2fl oz)
olive oil

3 zucchinis, grated

METHOD

1. Preheat oven to 180°C (355°F, Gas Mark 4). Grease and flour a loaf tin.

2. Mix together flour, baking powder, bicarb, salt, pepper, cayenne, spring onions and cheese in a large bowl until well combined.

3. Beat eggs in a separate bowl. Add milk and oil. Stir well.

4. Add zucchini to eggs and stir well.

5. Add zucchini and eggs to the dry ingredients, stirring until well combined, but not over-mixed.

6. Transfer to loaf tin.

7. Bake for 45 minutes, or until a skewer inserted in the centre comes out clean.

8. Allow to cool for 15 minutes before turning out onto a wire rack to cool completely.

GLUTEN-FREE PIZZA

INGREDIENTS

Pizza Base

¼ cup (50g, 2oz) chia seeds

¾ cup (185ml, 6fl oz) water

3 tbsps buckwheat flour (gluten free)

1 tsp dried mixed herbs

1 tsp salt

1 tbsp pine nuts, roughly chopped

2 tbsps pepitas, roughly chopped

Topping

2 fresh tomatoes, sliced

50g (2oz) feta cheese, crumbled

3-4 button mushrooms, thinly sliced

½ red onion, thinly sliced

Handful of basil leaves, torn

METHOD

1. Preheat oven to 180°C (350°F, Gas Mark 4) and line a baking tray with greaseproof paper.

2. Combine chia seeds, water, buckwheat flour, herbs and salt in a large bowl and mix well. Leave to stand for 15 minutes until the mixture starts to thicken. Add chopped pine nuts and pumpkin seeds and stir well.

3. Spread out the base mix on a piece of greaseproof paper and form the dough in a large oval. Flatten to about 1cm (½ in) for a firm, thin crust.

4. Place in the oven and bake for 20 minutes until base is firm and golden at the edges.

5. Remove from oven. Add tomato, feta cheese, mushrooms, onion and basil and return to the oven. Bake for an additional 10 minutes. Remove and cool slightly before serving.

KALE CHIPS

INGREDIENTS

1 bunch kale,
washed and dried

1 tbsp olive oil

1 tsp salt

METHOD

1. Preheat oven to 175°C (350°F, Gas Mark 4).

2. Line a baking tray.

3. Remove stems from kale.

4. Cut or tear leaves into bite-sized pieces.

5. Place on baking tray in an even layer and drizzle with olive oil. Rub
   the oil into the kale leaves using hands.

6. Season with salt.

7. Bake for 10 minutes, until edges of kale are lightly golden,
   but not burnt.

SUN-DRIED TOMATO TART

INGREDIENTS

Pie crust

1¼ cups (155g, 5oz) plain flour or wholmeal flour

½ tsp salt

75g (3oz) vegetable shortening, chilled

50g (2oz) unsalted butter, chilled and cubed

¼ cup (60ml, 2fl oz) cold water

Filling

4 eggs

1 cup (250ml, 8fl oz) milk

1 cup (160g, 6oz) sun-dried tomatoes

½ tsp olive oil

1 tsp garlic, minced

120g (4oz) goat's cheese, crumbled

Salt and pepper, to season

½ cup (60g, 2oz) Parmesan cheese, finely grated

METHOD

1. Mix together the flour, salt, shortening and butter. Cut the butter into the flour until a coarse crumb texture forms.

2. Add water a tablespoon at a time. Stop adding water when the dough forms large clumps.

3. Place dough on a floured work surface and fold into itself until well combined.

4. Divide dough in half and roll two round discs. Cover in plastic warp and chill in fridge for at least 2 hours.

5. When ready to assemble pie, preheat oven to 180°C (355°F, Gas Mark 4).

6. Remove pie crust from fridge and re-work dough by rolling out and folding over itself. Repeat until dough is pliable and press into a greased pie dish.

7. Blind bake pie crust for 10 minutes.

8. Meanwhile, whisk together eggs and milk. Stir in sun-dried tomatoes, oil, garlic and cheese. Season with salt and pepper.

9. Remove pie crust from oven and pour in egg mixture. Sprinkle cheese over the top.

10. Return to the oven to bake for 50 minutes, until egg is set and pastry is golden. Let sit for 5 minutes before serving.

POWER NUTBREAD

INGREDIENTS

1¼ cups (110g, 3¾ oz) oats

1 cup (125g, 4oz) flour, sifted

⅔ cup (140g, 5oz) Natvia or coconut sugar

1½ tsps baking powder

1 tsp bicarbonate of soda

¼ tsp salt

½ tsp cinnamon

½ tsp ground ginger

1 tbsp flax seeds

¼ cup (30g, 1oz) walnuts, coarsely chopped

¼ cup (30g, 1oz) pecans, coarsely chopped (reserve some whole for topping)

1 egg, beaten

2 ripe bananas

2 carrots, grated

85g (3oz) butter, melted

2 tbsps sugar-free peanut butter

1 tsp vanilla essence

1 tbsp lemon juice

METHOD

1. Preheat oven to 180°C (350°F, Gas Mark 4) and line a loaf tin with greaseproof paper.

2. Combine dry ingredients and nuts in a bowl. Set aside.

3. Place egg, banana, carrot, melted butter, peanut butter, vanilla and lemon juice in a large bowl and mix until well combined.

4. Add wet ingredients to dry ingredients and stir until just combined and all ingredients are moist.

5. Scrape into tin and smooth the surface with a spatula. Top with pecan halves.

6. Bake for 50 minutes or until a skewer inserted in the centre comes out clean.

PEANUT BUTTER COOKIES

INGREDIENTS

2 cups (250g, 8oz) plain flour

1½ tsp baking powder

½ tsp salt

1 tbsp unsalted butter, melted

2 egg whites

1 tsp vanilla extract

½ cup (180g, 6oz) soft sugar-free peanut butter

1 cup (155g, 5oz) coconut sugar

METHOD

1. Preheat oven to 180°C (355°F, Gas Mark 4). Line two baking trays.

2. Mix together flour, baking powder and salt. Set aside.

3. Whisk together butter, egg whites and vanilla. Mix in peanut butter and combine well. Stir in the coconut sugar.

4. Add peanut mixture to flour mix. Stir until well combined.

5. Using hands, roll balls from the dough.

6. Place each ball onto baking tray, flattening with fingers or the tines of a fork.

7. Place in the oven and bake for 10 minutes until golden.

8. Allow to cool for 10 minutes then transfer to a cooling wire.

RYE GALETTE WITH RICOTTA AND MUSHROOMS

INGREDIENTS

1 cup (110g, 4oz) rye flour

1 cup (125g, 4oz) whole wheat flour

1 tsp salt

170g (6oz) unsalted butter, chilled, diced

8 tbsps cold water

1 tsp apple cider vinegar

1 cup (190g, 7oz) ricotta cheese

½ cup (100g, 3oz) cream cheese

1 egg

1 egg, separated

12 button mushrooms, thinly sliced

Handful of sage leaves, to garnish

METHOD

1. Sift flours and salt over a large bowl.

2. Add butter and rub with fingers until mixture resembles rough breadcrumbs.

3. Add water. Work into a dough ball, adding more water if needed. Cover dough ball in plastic wrap and refrigerate for 1 hour.

4. When chilled, roll dough flat, then fold in on itself so it has three layers. Wrap dough in plastic and chill again for 1 hour.

5. Preheat the oven to 190°C (375°F, Gas Mark 5).

6. Stir together the vinegar, cheeses, egg and egg yolk.

7. Divide the dough in half, keeping unused dough in fridge. Roll the dough into circle and transfer to a lined tart dish, leaving a large overhang.

8. Spread half the cheese and egg filling on top of dough, then fold in edges to create a border. Arrange mushrooms on top. Repeat for remaining dough and filling.

9. Brush crust with egg white and bake for 25 minutes until filling has set and crust is golden.

10. Serve warm and garnish with sage leaves.

SERVES 8 ★ PREP 15MIN (PLUS SOAKING) ★ COOK TIME 40MIN

WHOLESOME NUT AND SEED LOAF

INGREDIENTS

1 cup (125g, 4oz) sunflower seeds

¼ cup (40g, 3oz) flaxseed

2 tbsps chia seeds

4 tbsps psyllium seed husks

½ cup (60g, 2oz) hazelnuts

1½ cups (130g, 4½ oz) rolled oats

1 tsp salt

Pinch of stevia

3 tbsps coconut oil, melted

1½ cups (375ml, 13fl oz) water

METHOD

1. Place the seeds, nuts, oats, salt and stevia in a large bowl and stir to combine.

2. Whisk together the oil and water and add to the dry ingredients.

3. Mix until all dry ingredients are coated and the mixture is thick.

4. Grease and line a loaf tin.

5. Transfer mixture in a loaf tin. Allow to sit overnight.

6. Preheat oven to 175°C (350°F, Gas Mark 4).

7. Bake for 40 minutes, or until loaf sounds hollow when tapped.

8. Allow to cool in the tin on a wire rack before slicing.

SERVES 4 ★ PREP 20MIN ★ COOK TIME 10MIN

BROCCOLI AND CORN QUESADILLA

INGREDIENTS

1 zucchini, grated, salted and drained

2 corn cobs, kernels removed and cooked

½ red onion, chopped

2 jalapeño peppers, seeds removed, chopped

1 head of broccoli, florets finely chopped

½ tsp salt

¼ tsp pepper

2 cups (250g, 8oz) cheddar cheese, grated

8 flour tortillas

Olive oil, for cooking

METHOD

1. Preheat oven to 100°C (210°F, Gas Mark ¼).

2. Mix together the zucchini, corn, onion, jalapeños, broccoli, salt and pepper.

3. Toss through cheese until well combined.

4. Evenly distribute filling onto tortillas and fold to contain.

5. Heat a splash of oil over a medium heat and gently fry a quesadilla for 2 minutes on each side, until lightly golden and cheese inside has melted.

6. Repeat with remaining quesadillas, transferring to a lined baking tray to keep warm in the oven.

BEEF SOBA NOODLES

INGREDIENTS

100g (3½ oz) soba noodles

¼ cup (60ml, 2fl oz) peanut oil

3 tbsps tamari (or soy sauce)

1½ tbsps toasted sesame oil

1½ tbsps rice wine vinegar

Pinch of stevia

225g (8oz, ½ lb) flank steak, trimmed and sliced

1 head of broccoli, broken into florets

1 carrot, finely jullienned

2 spring onions, sliced

Handful of coriander leaves

1 red chilli, seeds removed, thinly sliced

Sesame seeds, to garnish

METHOD

1. Bring a saucepan of water to the boil and add soba noodles. Remove from heat and let noodles soak for 3 minutes, then drain. Toss through peanut oil and set noodles aside.

2. In a small bowl, mix together tamari, sesame oil, rice wine vinegar and stevia and set aside.

3. Cook beef slices in oil in a frying pan over a medium-high heat for 1 minute, until no longer pink inside. Remove from heat and set aside.

4. Add a tablespoon of oil to the frying pan and saute broccoli, carrot and onion for 3 minutes, until softened.

5. Reduce heat and add beef and noodles to the pan and stir. Add soy mixture and toss through for 3 minutes.

6. Garnish with coriander, chilli and sesame seeds to serve.

TAHINI DRESSING

INGREDIENTS

Juice of 1 lemon

1 garlic clove, minced

½ cup (125ml, 4fl oz) water

½ cup (180g, 6oz) tahini

1 tsp maple syrup

1 tbsp apple cider vinegar

1½ tsps tamari (or soy sauce)

1 tsp ground coriander

1 tsp ground cumin

2 tbsps olive oil

¼ tsp salt

1 tbsp sesame seeds

METHOD

1. Puree lemon juice, garlic and water in a blender for 30 seconds.

2. Add tahini, maple syrup, vinegar, tamari, coriander, cumin and oil and blend until creamy.

3. Sprinkle with sesame seeds.

ASPARAGUS TART

INGREDIENTS

1 bunch of asparagus

Olive oil, for brushing

2½ cups (625g, 20oz) ricotta, drained

½ cup (60g, 2oz) mozzarella, grated

½ cup (60g, 2oz) grated asiago

2 garlic cloves, minced

2 eggs

3-4 pre-made shortcrust pastry shells

3-4 cherry tomatoes

½ cup (60g, 2oz) Parmesan cheese, finely grated

METHOD

1. Preheat oven to 205°C (400°F, Gas Mark 6).

2. Place asparagus on a baking tray, brush with oil and roast for 10 minutes, or until tender. Set aside.

3. Mix cheeses, except Parmesan, garlic and eggs in a large bowl until well combined.

4. Spoon cheese and egg mix into pastry shells. Arrange asparagus spears on top of tart. Push a tomato into each tart.

5. Sprinkle top with Parmesan cheese.

6. Bake for 15 minutes, until filling has set and crust is golden.

7. Allow to cool before serving

FLAX AND SESAME SEED CRACKERS

INGREDIENTS

4 tbsps flaxseed

4 tbsps white and black sesame seeds

½ cup (100g, 3oz) cooked quinoa

½ cup (60g, 2oz) quinoa flour (or brown rice flour)

¾ cup (60g, 2oz) quinoa flakes

½ cup (100g, 3oz) potato starch

1 tsp baking powder

1 tsp xanthan gum

1 tsp salt

100g (3oz) butter, softened

¼ cup (60ml, 2fl oz) olive oil

Very cold water, as required

Sesame and flaxseed, to finish

METHOD

1. Preheat oven to 205°C (400°F, Gas Mark 6). Line a baking tray.

2. Pulse flaxseed and sesame seeds in a food processor until crushed, but not creamy.

3. Add the cooked quinoa, quinoa flour, quinoa flakes, potato starch, baking powder, xanthan gum and salt to the food processor and blend well.

4. Add softened butter and oil and pulse to combine. If dough appears too dry, add a drop of water at a time.

5. Transfer dough to baking tray and roll out thinly to fill tray.

6. Push extra flax and sesame seeds onto the surface of the dough.

7. Place in the oven to bake for 20 minutes until golden and firm.

8. Cool on a wire rack before slicing into crackers.

GREEN PEA FRITTERS

INGREDIENTS

400g (14oz) fresh peas

1¼ cups (155g, 5oz)
self-raising flour

3 eggs

1 spring onion, finely
chopped

2 tbsps chopped parsley

80g (3oz) feta cheese,
crumbled

Salt and pepper

Olive oil, for frying

Plain yoghurt, to serve

METHOD

1. Bring a saucepan of salted water to the boil. Cook peas on a rolling boil for 4 minutes. Remove from heat and drain.

2. Blend the flour, eggs, spring onion and half of the peas in a food processor until combined.

3. Add remaining peas, parsley and feta and pulse gently to combine. Season with salt and pepper.

4. Form into patties using your hands.

5. Heat the olive oil in a large frying pan. Add patties and fry for 2 minutes on each side until golden brown.

6. Serve warm, accompanied by yoghurt.

SERVES 2 ★ PREP 15MIN ★ COOK TIME 10MIN

BLACK BEAN DIP

INGREDIENTS

¼ cup (60ml, 2fl oz) olive oil

2 onions, chopped

4 cloves garlic, roughly chopped

2 jalapeño peppers, seeded and chopped

2 x 400g (14oz) cans black beans, rinsed and drained

1½ tsps salt

½ tsp ground cumin

Juice of 1 lime

3 tbsps water

¼ cup (10g, ¼ oz) coriander, chopped

Salt and pepper, to taste

METHOD

1. Saute onions, garlic and jalapeño peppers in oil over a medium heat for 10 minutes until soft.

2. Transfer to a food processer and blend to desired consistency.

3. Add black beans, salt, cumin, lime juice, water and coriander and blend until well combined.

4. Season with salt and pepper, to taste.

STEAMED MUSSELS IN WHITE WINE SAUCE

INGREDIENTS

1kg (2lb) mussels, debearded

½ cup (125ml, 4fl oz) dry white wine

2 spring onions, finely chopped

1 clove garlic, minced

2 tbsps butter

2 tsps plain flour

1 bunch flat leaf parsley, chopped

METHOD

1. Place mussels and white wine in a large saucepan and bring to the boil. Reduce heat to low and cover pot. Cook for 5-7 minutes, until mussel shells have opened.

2. Remove mussels and retain cooking liquid.

3. Sieve cooking liquid to remove any grit. Set aside.

4. Saute spring onions and garlic in butter in a saucepan for 5 minutes over a medium heat until soft.

5. Add flour and stir well.

6. Mix in mussel cooking liquid and stir on a medium heat until sauce thickens.

7. Add parsley and stir through.

8. To serve, place mussels in a serving bowl and pour sauce over top.

FETA AND SPINACH PANCAKES

INGREDIENTS

4 eggs

1 cup (250ml, 8fl oz)
thickened cream

3 tbsps melted butter

1 cup (250ml, 8fl oz)
soda water

1½ cups (185g, 6oz)
plain flour

Pinch of salt

1 egg white, beaten
to soft peaks

Filling

1 clove garlic, minced

2 tsps butter

900g (2lb) baby spinach

125g (4oz) feta,
crumbled

½ cup (60g, 2oz)
Parmesan cheese,
grated

1 cup (125g, 4oz)
pine nuts, toasted

METHOD

1. Preheat oven to 205°C (400°F, Gas Mark 6).

2. Combine eggs, cream, butter and soda water in a bowl. Add flour
   and salt and whisk until mixture is smooth. Gently fold in egg whites.
   Allow to rest for 15 minutes.

3. Heat oil in a frying pan over a medium heat and pour in half the
   batter. Fry for 2 minutes on each side until golden. Repeat with
   remaining batter. Remove pancakes from heat. Set aside.

4. Saute garlic in butter for 3 minutes until soft. Add the spinach and
   cook for 1-2 minutes until soft. Add cheeses and pine nuts and stir to
   combine.

5. Spoon spinach mix onto the pancakes and roll up.

6. Reheat rolled pancakes in oven before serving.

SAVOURY MILLET PORRIDGE

INGREDIENTS

½ cup (60g, 2oz) millet

½ cup (125ml, 4fl oz) water

1 tbsp oil

½ tsp mustard seeds

3 curry leaves

1 clove garlic, minced

1 onion, finely chopped

1 tsp green chilli, minced

¾ cup (175g, 6oz) tomato puree

¼ tsp ground turmeric

Salt, to taste

Handful flat-leaf parsley, to serve

METHOD

1. Place millet in a frying pan over a medium-high heat and dry roast for 2-3 minutes. Add water and bring to the boil. Reduce heat and cover. Cook until water has fully absorbed. Set side for 2-3 minutes, then fluff up with a fork.

2. Heat oil in a frying pan over a medium heat and add mustard seeds, curry leaves, garlic, onions and green chilli. Saute for 5 minutes until onion is soft.

3. Add tomato puree, turmeric and salt to the pan and cook on medium heat for 5 minutes.

4. Add the cooked millet and cook, stirring, until heated through.

5. Garnish with parsley to serve.

QUINOA FRITTERS WITH POACHED EGGS

INGREDIENTS

½ cup (85g, 3oz) quinoa, rinsed well

¼ cup (60ml, 2fl oz) olive oil

1 potato, coarsely grated

1 onion, finely chopped

1 tsp fennel seeds

2 eggs, beaten

¼ cup (30g, 1oz) plain flour

Bunch of flat leaf parsley, leaves chopped (retain some for garnish)

4 eggs

2 tsps white vinegar

METHOD

1. Bring a saucepan of salted water to the boil and cook quinoa for 15 minutes, until tender. Drain and set aside.

2. Meanwhile, in a tablespoon of oil saute grated potato, onion and fennel seeds on a medium heat for 3 minutes, or until potato is tender.

3. Add potato mixture, beaten eggs, flour and parsley to the quinoa. Season with salt and pepper. Stir well until combined.

4. Heat oil in a frying pan on medium-high heat.

5. Spoon out a quarter of the batter and fry fritter for 5 minutes, then turn over and fry for 2 minutes until golden. Repeat with remaining mixture. Fry in batches dependent on pan size.

6. To poach eggs, quarter fill a large frying pan with water and bring to a bare simmer.

7. Crack an egg into a small bowl and gently slip it into the water. Repeat with each egg.

8. Add vinegar to the water. Turn off heat and cover frying pan. Allow eggs to cook for 4 minutes, until whites have set.

9. Serve fritters with poached egg on top. Garnish with parsley.

CHICKEN FRITTATA

INGREDIENTS

Olive oil, for frying

1 chicken breast,
cut into small pieces

1 head of broccoli florets,
finely chopped

1 yellow capsicum,
diced

3 spring onions,
finely chopped

2 cloves garlic, minced

½ tsp salt

¼ tsp pepper

8 eggs

½ cup (60g, 2oz)
cheddar cheese, grated

Bunch of dill, finely
chopped (reserve
some for garnish)

METHOD

1. Preheat oven to 180°C (355°F, Gas Mark 4). Lightly grease a pie dish.

2. Heat oil in a large frying pan over a medium heat.

3. Fry chicken for 3-4 minutes until lightly golden and cooked through. Remove from heat and set aside.

4. Heat oil in frying pan over a medium heat. Saute broccoli and capsicum for 5 minutes, until softening.

5. Add spring onions, garlic, salt and pepper and cook for 1 minute. Remove from heat and set aside.

6. Whisk eggs In a large bowl.

7. Add cheese, chicken, broccoli, capsicum and dill.

8. Pour egg and chicken mix into pie dish.

9. Bake for 40 minutes, until set and a skewer inserted into centre comes out clean.

10. Let rest for 5 minutes before serving. Garnish with dill, to serve.

BROAD BEAN PATTIES

INGREDIENTS

200g (7oz) cooked broad beans

200g (7oz) cooked peas

Handful of dill, finely chopped

1 tbsp tamari (or soy sauce)

¾ cup (90g, 3oz) breadcrumbs

1 egg

Oil, for cooking

Plain yoghurt, to serve

Sprig of dill, to garnish

METHOD

1. Blend beans, peas, dill and tamari in a food processor until smooth.

2. Add breadcrumbs and egg and pulse until well combined.

3. Remove and form into patties using hands.

4. Heat oil in frying pan over a medium heat and fry a pattie for 5 minutes on each siide, or until heated through and golden brown. Repeat with remaining mixture.

5. Serve hot with yoghurt and garnished with dill.

SERVES 4 ★ PREP 10MIN

AVOCADO HUMMUS

INGREDIENTS

1 x 400g (14 oz) can chickpeas, drained

3 tbsps olive oil

1½ tbsps tahini

3 tbsps fresh lime juice

1 clove garlic, peeled

Salt and pepper

Pinch of ground cumin

2 ripe avocados, cored and peeled

Few coriander leaves, to garnish

METHOD

1. Combine chickpeas, olive oil, tahini, lime juice and garlic in a food processer and pulse for 2 minutes until smooth.

2. Season with salt and pepper.

3. Add cumin and avocado. Pulse for 2 minutes until smooth and creamy. Add additional lime juice, tahini or oil to taste.

4. Spoon into a serving bowl and garnish with coriander.

DATE, NUT AND CHOCOLATE BARS

INGREDIENTS

1 cup (125g, 4oz) walnuts

⅓ cup (60g, 2oz) chia seeds

⅓ cup (60g, 2oz) ground flaxseed

⅓ cup (60g, 2oz) hemp seeds

¼ cup (40g, 1½ oz) cacao nibs

¼ cup (20g, ¾ oz) coconut flakes

¾ cup (150g, 5oz) sunflower seeds

1 cup (160g, 6oz) dates

½ cup (80g, 3oz) raisins

Coconut oil, melted, if needed

METHOD

1. Pulse dry ingredients in a food processor until well combined and a coarse powder forms.

2. Add dates and rasins and pulse until mixture becomes sticky. Add coconut oil if mixture is too dry.

3. Transfer mixture to a lined shallow baking dish and press into dish.

4. Refrigerate for at least 1 hour, until set.

5. Cut into bars to serve.

CASHEW OAT BARS

INGREDIENTS

1½ cup (130g, 4½ oz) quick oats

½ cup (40g, 1½ oz) oat bran

½ cup (40g, 1½ oz) desiccated coconut

½ cup (60g, 2oz) cashews, chopped finely

½ tsp salt

60g (2oz) cashew butter

1 tbsp coconut oil

¼ cup (90g, 3oz) rice malt syrup

Handful cashews, to garnish

METHOD

1. Mix together the oats, oat bran, desiccated coconut, chopped cashews and salt in a large bowl.

2. In a saucepan over a low-medium heat, gently melt cashew butter, coconut oil and rice malt syrup and stir until combined.

3. Remove from heat when starting to bubble and pour into dry ingredients.

4. Stir wet and dry ingredients until well combined.

5. Transfer mixture to a lined baking dish. Press into dish and smooth top with a spatula.

6. Refrigerate for at least 4 hours.

7. When set, remove from baking dish and cut into bars.

8. Garnish with whole cashews.

PUMPKIN OAT COOKIES

INGREDIENTS

200g (7oz) butter, softened

½ cup (110g, 4oz) coconut sugar

1 cup (225g, 8oz) pumpkin, mashed

1 egg

1 tsp vanilla extract

2 cups (250g, 8oz) whole wheat or plain flour

1 cup (90g, 3oz) oats

1 tsp ground cinnamon

1 tsp bicarbonate of soda

½ tsp baking powder

1 tsp salt

METHOD

1. Preheat oven to 190°C (375°F, Gas Mark 5).

2. Using a hand-held electric mixer, beat butter and sugar until creamy and combined.

3. Add pumpkin, egg and vanilla and beat until smooth.

4. Place flour, oats, cinnamon, bicarb, baking powder and salt in a separate bowl and stir to combine.

5. Fold creamed butter and pumpkin into dry ingredients.

6. Spoon 2 tablespoons of batter per cookie onto a lined baking tray. Flatten slightly and shape into rounds.

7. Place in the oven and bake for 15 minutes, until golden.

8. Remove from the oven and place on a wire rack to cool.

CHOCOLATE AND BEETROOT MUFFINS

INGREDIENTS

2 tbsps flaxseed meal

5 tbsps water

2 large beetroots, roasted, peeled and pureed

¼ cup (60ml, 2fl oz) coconut oil, melted

¼ cup (90g, 3oz) maple syrup

1 tsp stevia

1½ tsps bicarbonate of soda

¼ tsp salt

¼ cup (60ml, 2fl oz) almond milk

½ cup (60g, 2oz) unsweetened cocoa powder

1⅓ cups (165g, 5½ oz) wholemeal flour

Pinch of icing sugar, to dust (optional)

METHOD

1. Preheat oven to 190°C (375°F, Gas Mark 5). Grease and line 12 muffin cups.

2. Combine flaxseed and water in a large bowl and allow to soak for 5 minutes.

3. Add beetroot puree, coconut oil, maple syrup, stevia, bicarb and salt and mix well.

4. Add almond milk and whisk.

5. Add cocoa powder and flour. Mix until combined.

6. Divide evenly among muffin cups.

7. Bake for 20 minutes, until a skewer inserted in the centre comes out clean.

8. Allow to cool slightly before serving.

9. Serve with a light dust of icing sugar, if desired.

SESAME DATE BLISS BALLS

INGREDIENTS

1 tbsp coconut oil

1 cup (160g, 6oz) pitted dates

¹/₃ cup (120g, 4oz) sesame seeds

½ cup (180g, 6oz) cashew nuts

¼ cup (20g, ¾oz) sunflower seeds

¼ cup (20g, ¾oz) flax seeds

1 tbsp honey (optional)

METHOD

1. Combine all ingredients in a food processor and blend until nuts are chopped finely and ingredients are well combined.

2. Roll a ball by hand using a tablespoon of mixture.

3. Place ball on a lined tray or plate.

4. Repeat with remaining mixture.

   Note: Serve immediately, or store in a sealed container in the fridge for up to 20 days.

SERVES 6 ★ PREP 15MIN ★ COOK TIME 50MIN

LEMON AND LIME CAKE

INGREDIENTS

125g unsalted butter, room temperature

1 cup (350g, 12oz) rice malt syrup

1 tbsp lemon rind, finely grated

1 tbsp lime rind, finely grated

2 eggs, beaten

1 cup (125g, 4oz) self-raising flour

¾ cup (60g, 2oz) desiccated coconut

1 cup (250ml, 8fl oz) milk

METHOD

1. Preheat oven to 180°C (355°F, Gas Mark 4). Grease and line a loaf tin.

2. Combine butter and rice malt syrup together with a whisk or electric mixer.

3. Add grated lemon and lime rinds.

4. Beat in eggs, one at a time, until thoroughly combined.

5. Gently fold in flour, coconut and milk until combined.

6. Spoon batter into loaf tin.

7. Bake for 50 minutes, or until golden and a skewer inserted in the centre comes out clean.

PEANUT BUTTER BARS

INGREDIENTS

235g (8oz) butter

120g (4oz) peanut butter

1 cup (125g, 4oz)
almond flour

1¼ cups (310ml, 10fl oz)
powdered erythritol

55g (2oz) butter

115g (4oz) dark
chocolate, chopped

METHOD

1. Combine butter, peanut butter, almond flour and powdered erythritol in a medium saucepan over a low heat.

2. Cook, stirring constantly, for 3-5 minutes, until all ingredients have dissolved and combined.

3. Pour the mixture into a glass or ceramic baking dish and transfer to the refrigerator to chill for 45 minutes.

4. Meanwhile, place the butter and chocolate in a medium saucepan over a very low heat. Cook, stirring constantly, until chocolate has melted.

5. Remove the baking dish from the refrigerator and spread the chocolate layer evenly over the top, using a spatula to smooth.

6. Return to the refrigerator to chill overnight.

7. When chilled, cut into squares and serve. Store any leftovers in the refrigerator.

DINNER AND SIDES

Sprouts with pork and peanuts   126

Grilled salmon with tartare sauce   128

Cauliflower rice   129

Fish Baked with lemon and thyme   130

Prawns with spaghetti and pistachio pesto   132

Zucchini fries with chive yoghurt dip   133

Meatballs with zucchini pasta   134

Bombay chicken and potatoes   136

Almond crusted chicken tenders   137

Baked chicken rolls with mushrooms   138

Coconut prawn curry   140

Lime rice salad   142

Lemon dill Coleslaw   143

Eggplant and white bean balls   144

Spiced lamb cutlets   146

Coconut and lime chicken   147

Meatloaf with honey glaze   148

Grilled eggplant   150

Grilled marinated steak   152

Chimichurri sauce   153

Moroccan spiced mince with couscous   154

Spicy Mexican chilli   156

Roasted turkey with peppercorns   157

Roasted pork chops with garlic and sage   158

Chicken tikka masala   160

Sesame crusted chicken   161

Meatballs with tahini sauce   162

Lemon baked salmon   164

Quinoa and corn burritos   165

SPROUTS WITH PORK AND PEANUTS

INGREDIENTS

450g (1lb) pork tenderloin, trimmed and sliced

1 tbsp cornflour

5 tbsps tamari (or soy sauce), divided

2 tbsps rice wine vinegar

1 tbsp coconut sugar

1 tbsp Chinese rice wine

2 tbsps water

Vegetable or peanut oil, for frying

4 tbsps unsalted peanuts

400g (14oz) Brussels sprouts, trimmed and halved

Small piece of ginger, grated

2 garlic cloves, thinly sliced

½ tsp chilli flakes

METHOD

1. In a medium bowl, mix cornflour with 2 tablespoons of tamari. Add meat and toss until coated. Set aside for 5 minutes.

2. Mix remaining tamari with vinegar, coconut sugar, rice wine and water together in a small bowl. Set aside.

3. Heat a tablespoon of oil in frying pan or wok over a medium-high heat and fry the peanuts for 2 minutes, until golden. Set aside.

4. Add another tablespoon of oil to frying pan. When hot, add pork and stir-fry for 4 minutes, until browned, but not fully cooked through. Set aside.

5. Add another tablspoon of oil to frying pan and stir-fry sprouts for 5 minutes, until charred and tender. Add a splash of water after 4 minutes to steam cook.

6. Add another tablespoon of oil and saute ginger, garlic and chilli for 1 minute.

7. Return pork to the pan. Pour in tamari mix and simmer for 5 minutes, until sauce thickens and pork cooks through.

GRILLED SALMON WITH TARTARE SAUCE

INGREDIENTS

4 salmon fillets

Olive oil, for brushing

Salt and pepper

2 bunches of spinach, leaves picked

Tartare sauce

½ cup (125ml, 4fl oz) mayonnaise

2 tbsps pickles, roughly chopped

1 tbsp white wine vinegar

1 tbsp capers

1 tsp wholegrain mustard

METHOD

1. Heat grill to a medium-high heat.

2. Lightly brush salmon with oil and place under grill to cook for 5 minutes each side.

3. Season with salt and pepper and set aside, covered to keep warm.

4. To make the tartare sauce place all the ingredients in a food processor. Pulse until sauce is finely chopped but still textured.

5. Serve on a bed of spinach, wilted for 1-2 minutes in a saucepan over medium heat.

SERVES 4 ★ PREP 20MIN ★ COOK TIME 10MIN

CAULIFLOWER RICE

INGREDIENTS

1 cauliflower head, broken into florets

1 tbsp sesame oil

1 tbsp freshly grated ginger

¼ tsp pepper

1 tbsp vegetable oil

2 cloves garlic, minced

1 onion, finely diced

2 carrots, peeled and finely diced

1 zucchini, finely diced

2 spring onions, thinly sliced

Flat leaf parsley, to garnish

METHOD

1. Place cauliflower florets in a food processor and pulse for 2-3 minutes until it looks likes rice. Set aside.

2. Whisk together the sesame oil, ginger and pepper in a small bowl and set aside.

3. Heat vegetable oil in a large frying pan or wok over a medium heat. Add garlic and onion and saute for 4 minutes until soft.

4. Add carrot and zucchini and cook for 3 minutes.

5. Stir in cauliflower and spring onions and cook for 3 minutes.

6. Toss through sesame oil. Serve warm and garnish with parsley.

SERVES 2 ★ PREP 10MIN ★ COOK TIME 15MIN

FISH BAKED WITH LEMON AND THYME

INGREDIENTS

1 onion, sliced

2 firm white fish fillets
such as snapper or cod

½ lemon, juiced

2 tbsps olive oil

Pinch of salt

Pinch of pepper

1-2 tsps thyme leaves
(or 1 tbsp dried thyme)

½ lemon, sliced

1 tomato, sliced

1 small capsicum, sliced

METHOD

1. Preheat oven to 190°C (375°F, Gas Mark 5) and line a chopping board
   with brown paper. (You can also use greaseproof paper
   or an ovenproof dish with a lid for this recipe).

2. Place the onion slices in a strip in the centre of the brown paper.

3. Wash the fish and pat dry with paper towels. Place the fish over the
   onion and squeeze lemon juice over the fish. Drizzle over the olive oil.

4. Rub the fish with salt and pepper and sprinkle with thyme leaves.

5. Place lemon, tomato and capsicum slices on top of the fish.

6. Fold the brown paper over the top of the fish and wrap until a snug
   parcel is formed. Tie up the ends with string.

7. Place in the oven and bake for 15-20 minutes, depending on the type
   and size of fish.

PRAWNS WITH SPAGHETTI AND PISTACHIO PESTO

INGREDIENTS

400g (14oz) spaghetti

1 clove garlic, minced

½ tsp salt

½ bunch of basil leaves, (retaining few for garnish)

¼ bunch of parsley

¼ bunch of mint

½ cup (60g, 2oz) toasted, unsalted pistachios

1 tbsp Parmesan cheese, finely grated

3 tbsps olive oil

1 tbsp lemon juice

Salt and pepper, to season

700g (1½ lb) green king prawns, peeled and deveined, tails intact

METHOD

1. Bring a large saucepan of salted water to the boil and cook spaghetti until al dente. Drain.

2. Meanwhile, using a mortar and pestle or food processor, grind garlic, salt, basil, parlsey and mint and grind until a thick paste forms. Add the pistachios and pound or process until creamy.

3. Mix in Parmesan cheese, olive oil and lemon juice.

4. Season with salt and pepper.

5. Pan fry the prawns over a medium heat for 1-2 minutes on each side until opaque and cooked through.

6. Transfer pasta to a large serving bowl.

7. Toss pesto through the pasta. Toss prawns through the pasta.

8. Serve with a garnish of basil leaves.

SERVES 4 ★ PREP 20MIN ★ COOK TIME 10MIN

ZUCCHINI FRIES WITH CHIVE YOGHURT DIP

INGREDIENTS

Olive oil, for greasing

1 tsp mixed dried herbs

1½ tbsps plain flour

¾ tsp salt

¾ cup (90g, 3oz) breadcrumbs

2 egg whites

2 zucchinis

Yoghurt dip

1 garlic clove, minced

1 tsp lemon rind, finely grated

⅓ cup (10g, ¼ oz) fresh chives, chopped (retain a few for garnish)

1½ cup (240g, 12oz) plain Greek yoghurt

METHOD

1. Preheat oven to 220°C. Grease baking tray with olive oil.

2. In a bowl, mix together dried herbs, flour and salt.

3. Place breadcrumbs in second bowl.

4. In a third bowl, whip egg whites to frothy, almost soft peaks.

5. Slice zucchini in quarters lengthwise, and then halve crosswise.

6. Dunk each zucchini stick into flour mix, then dip into egg white, then in breadcrumbs. Repeat for remaining zucchini fries.

7. Place coated zucchini on baking tray and place in the oven. Bake for 10 minutes, turning once, until crispy golden.

8. To make the dip, place garlic, lemon rind, chives and yoghurt in a bowl. Season with salt and pepper. Stir to combine. Serve garnished with retained chives.

MEATBALLS WITH ZUCCHINI PASTA

INGREDIENTS

250g (9oz) pork mince

250g (9oz) veal mince

1 onion, finely diced

1 garlic clove, minced

1 tbsp olive oil

½ cup (60g, 2oz) Parmesan cheese, grated

1 egg

Salt and pepper, to taste

4 zucchinis, trimmed and sliced into long, thin strips

1 cup (250ml, 8fl oz) thickened cream

Small handful of grated Parmesan cheese, for pasta

15-20 cherry tomatoes

10-15 basil leaves

¾ cup (90g, 3oz) pine nuts

½ cup (60g, 2oz) Parmesan cheese, sliced, to serve

METHOD

1. Place mince, onion, garlic, olive oil, grated cheese, egg, salt and pepper in a bowl. Mix with hands until well combined.

2. Form small balls of the mince mixture. Place in a bowl, cover, and refrigerate for 10 minutes.

3. Heat oil in a frying pan on a medium heat. Fry meatballs for 15 minutes, until brown and cooked through.

4. Place zucchini strips in a saucepan. Add cream and heat over a low-medium heat for 3 minutes, until heated through.

5. Transfer zucchini to a serving bowl. Toss through Parmesan cheese.

6. Add cherry tomatoes, basil leaves, meatballs and pine nuts and mix to combine.

7. Season with salt and pepper. Top with slices of Parmesan.

BOMBAY CHICKEN AND POTATOES

INGREDIENTS

Oil, for frying

1 onion, finely chopped

800g (1¾ lb) chicken breasts or thighs, cut into bite-sized pieces

4 potatoes, cut into chunks

2 tbsps medium or hot curry powder

2 tbsps turmeric

1 tbsp ground cumin

1 tsp ground chilli

1½ tbsps paprika

Small piece of ginger, grated

Bunch of fresh coriander, including stalks, finely chopped (retain a sprig for garnish)

2 tomatoes, diced

½ cup (90g, 3oz) lentils

1²/₃ cups (400ml, 13fl oz) water

Salt and pepper, to season

METHOD

1. Heat 3 tablespoons of oil in a large frying pan over a medium-high heat. Add onion, chicken pieces, potatoes, spices, ginger and coriander and fry, stirring, for 3 minutes.

2. Add tomatoes and lentils and stir through for a further 2 minutes.

3. Add water and reduce heat to a simmer. Cook, covered, for 30 minutes, until chicken and potato are cooked through.

4. Season with salt and pepper. Garnish with coriander.

SERVES 4 ★ PREP 25MIN ★ COOK TIME 30MIN

ALMOND-CRUSTED CHICKEN TENDERS

INGREDIENTS

3 chicken breasts,
cut into bite-sized chunks

1¼ cups (150g, 5oz)
almond meal

1 tbsp paprika

1 tsp cayenne pepper

1 tsp black pepper

1 tsp salt

2 eggs

METHOD

1. Preheat oven to 235°C (455°F, Gas Mark 8). Grease and line
    a baking tray.

2. Mix almond meal, spices and salt and pepper in a bowl and transfer
    to a flat plate.

3. In a separate bowl, whisk eggs.

4. Cover a batch of chicken pieces with plastic wrap and pound
    to the desired thickness with meat tenderiser or rolling pin. Repeat
    until all chicken is prepared.

5. Dip chicken into eggs, then dip into almond mixture, fully coating.
    Repeat with all chicken pieces.

6. Place coated chicken pieces on baking dish.

7. Bake for 30 minutes, turning after 15 minutes, until golden.

BAKED CHICKEN ROLLS WITH MUSHROOMS

INGREDIENTS

2 tbsps olive oil

1 onion, finely chopped

450g (1lb) button mushrooms, finely chopped

1 red capsicum, finely diced

2 tsps paprika

Salt and pepper

Zest and juice of 1 lemon

1/3 cup (80ml, 3fl oz) unsweetened orange juice

4 boneless, skinless chicken breast halves

Fresh herbs, to garnish

METHOD

1. Preheat oven to 180°C (355°F, Gas Mark 4).

2. Heat oil in a frying pan over a medium heat. Add onion and fry, stirring, for 5 minutes until soft then add mushrooms and capsicum and fry for a further 5 minutes.

3. Add paprika and season with salt and pepper. Stir in lemon zest and juice. Cook for further 2-3 minutes until aromatic.

4. Add orange juice and cook for 2-3 minutes, until almost evapourated.

5. Slice the chicken almost in half lengthways and fold open.

6. Cover each piece with plastic wrap. Use a meat pounder or rolling pin to flatten to 1cm (½ in) thick. Cut into rectangles.

7. Place a spoonfull of filling inside each chicken rectangle and roll chicken lengthwise around filling. Secure with twine or a toothpick.

8. Heat oil on a medium heat and pan fry each roll until lightly golden.

9. When seared, place rolls onto a lined baking dish. Transfer to the oven and roast for 20 minutes, or until chicken is cooked through.

10. Slice rolls to serve. Garnish with herbs.

COCONUT PRAWN CURRY

INGREDIENTS

5 cloves garlic

5 dried red chillies

3 ripe tomatoes,
chopped

1 tsp cumin seeds

1 tsp salt

1 tbsp vinegar

1 tsp coconut sugar
(optional)

Olive oil, for frying

1 onion, finely chopped

½ cup (115g, 4oz)
red curry paste

1 cup (225g, 8oz)
tomato paste

2 cups (500ml, 1pt) fish
(or chicken) stock

1 x 400ml (14fl oz) can
coconut milk

20 green king prawns,
peeled and deveined,
tails intact

Coriander, to garnish

METHOD

1. Place the garlic, red chillies, tomatoes, cumin seeds, salt, vinegar and sugar, if using, in a food processor and pulse until a smooth paste forms.

2. Heat the oil in a deep frying pan over medium-high heat. Fry the onions for 5 minutes, until soft and golden (do not burn). Add the curry paste and fry for 2 minutes until aromatic. Add the tomato paste, stock and coconut milk.

3. Simmer on medium heat for 10 mins, then add the prawns. Cook for 3 mins or until opaque.

4. Serve in bowls with steamed rice, garnished with fresh coriander.

LIME RICE SALAD

INGREDIENTS

2 cups (310g, 8oz)
brown rice

1 lime, juiced

1 clove garlic, minced

1 tbsp olive oil

3 tbsps fresh coriander,
chopped

Salt and pepper, to taste

Lime slices, to garnish

METHOD

1. Cook brown rice in a saucepan of lightly salted water according to the directions on the packet. Drain when cooked. Set aside.

2. Meanwhile, whisk together lime juice with garlic and oil in a large bowl.

3. Add coriander and cooked rice to the dressing and toss until rice is well coated.

4. Season with salt and pepper, to taste, and garnish with lime slices.

LEMON DILL COLESLAW

INGREDIENTS

1 white cabbage, grated

1 cucumber, quartered and diced

1 spring onion, chopped

1 radish, halved and sliced

½ bunch of dill, chopped

4 tbsps sunflower oil

1½ tsps vinegar

1 tsp salt

1 lemon, juiced

Salt and pepper, to taste

METHOD

1   Prepare vegetables and place in a salad bowl. Add dill and mix to combine.

2. Whisk together oil, vinegar, salt and lemon juice.

3. Toss dressing through coleslaw until vegetables are well coated.

4. Season with salt and pepper.

EGGPLANT AND WHITE BEAN BALLS

INGREDIENTS

Olive oil, for frying

1 eggplant, diced

¼ tsp salt

½ tsp pepper

1 onion, finely chopped

¼ tsp cayenne pepper

2 cloves garlic, minced

2 cups (340g, 12oz) cooked cannellini beans

¼ cup (10g, ¼ oz) flat leaf parsley, chopped

Pinch of chilli flakes

¾ cup (90g, 3oz) breadcrumbs

METHOD

1. Preheat oven to 190°C (375°F, Gas Mark 5) and line a baking tray.

2. Heat a tablespoon of oil in a frying pan and saute eggplant for 5 minutes over a medium heat. Add more oil if required to prevent sticking.

3. Season with salt and pepper.

4. Add water to just cover the eggplant. Cook for 15 minutes, until tender. Set aside.

5. Heat a tablespoon of oil in the same pan. Add onion cayenne pepper and garlic and saute for 5 minutes, until soft.

6. Pulse eggplant, beans, parsley, chilli and the onion mixture in a food processor until well combined.

7. Add to a bowl with breadcrumbs and mix with hands until well combined.

8. Form small balls from the mixture and place on baking tray.

9. Bake for 15 minutes. Turn off oven and let cook for a further 20 minutes, until heated though and golden.

10. Serve on rice with tomato sauce. Garnish with parsley.

SPICED LAMB CUTLETS

INGREDIENTS

3 tbsps olive oil

1 tbsp fresh thyme

1 tsp cumin seeds

2 tsps fennel seeds

½ tsp ground coriander

½ tsp coarse salt

1 tsp peppercorns

12 lamb cutlets

2 tbsps lemon juice

Oil, for cooking

METHOD

1. Combine olive oil with thyme, cumin seeds, fennel seeds, coriander, salt and peppercorns in a small bowl. Place lamb cutlets on a plate and rub each side with the spice mixture.

2. Let cutlets sit in the marinade for a minimum for 30 minutes to 1 hour.

3. Preheat barbecue, pan or grill to hot.

4. Cook cutlets on one side until the first sign of moisture appears on top, about 3-4 minutes. Turn over, brush with the lemon juice and cook for a further 3 minutes for medium-rare, or longer to your preference. Turn once only.

5. Remove cutlets from heat.

6. Cover loosely with foil and rest for 2 minutes before serving.

COCONUT AND LIME CHICKEN

INGREDIENTS

6 tbsps coconut milk

2 tbsps fresh lime juice

1 tsp ground ginger

1 clove garlic, minced

1 tsp dried basil (or
1 tbsp fresh basil)

1 tbsp honey

½ tsp salt

1 tsp pepper

8 chicken drumsticks

Lime slices, to garnish

Coconut or plain rice,
to serve

METHOD

1. Preheat oven to 235°C (455°F, Gas Mark 8) and line a baking tray with greaseproof paper.

2. Mix together the coconut milk, lime juice, ginger, garlic, basil, honey, salt and pepper in a large bowl.

3. Toss chicken through mixture until well coated.

4. Place chicken on baking tray and cook for 30 minutes, until chicken is cooked through.

5. Garnish with lime slices and serve with rice.

SERVES 4 ★ PREP 20MIN ★ COOK TIME 55MIN

MEATLOAF WITH HONEY GLAZE

INGREDIENTS

500g (1lb 2oz) beef mince

1 cup (125g, 4oz) breadcrumbs

1 onion, finely chopped

1 carrot, finely diced

3 zucchinis, grated

4 pickles, chopped

2 tbsps tomato sauce

2 tbsps mixed dried herbs (or 1 tbsp dried oregano)

Salt and pepper, to taste

1 egg, lightly beaten

Glaze

1 cup (225g, 8oz) tomato paste

1 tbsp apple cider vinegar

¼ cup (90g, 3oz) honey

METHOD

1. Preheat oven to 180°C (350°F, Gas Mark 4) and line a baking tray with greaseproof paper.

2. Combine mince, breadcrumbs, onion, carrot, zucchini, pickles, tomato sauce, dried herbs, salt and pepper and egg in a large bowl. Mix well with hands.

3. Shape mince into a rectangle and place on baking tray.

4. Bake for 30 minutes until firm to touch. Remove any excess fat.

5. Combine the tomato paste, vinegar and honey in a small saucepan. Bring to a quick boil, then remove from heat. Spoon glaze on top of meatloaf.

6. Return to the oven for a further 10 minutes.

7. Stand on tray for 5 minutes before slicing and serving with the rest of the glaze as a sauce.

GRILLED EGGPLANT

INGREDIENTS

Yoghurt Sauce

1 cup (225g, 8oz)
plain Greek yoghurt

1 garlic clove, minced

1 tsp ground cumin

1 tbsp fresh lemon juice

2 tbsps tahini (optional)

¼ tsp salt

Pinch of pepper

Eggplant

3 large eggplants, halved

¼ cup (60ml, 2fl oz) olive
oil

¼ tsp salt

Pinch of pepper

To serve

½ pomegranate, seeds
only

1 tbsp mint leaves,
finely sliced

2 tbsps coriander, sliced

¼ cup (30g, 1oz) walnuts,
chopped

1 tbsp honey (optional)

METHOD

1. Place the sauce ingredients in a bowl and mix well to combine. Cover and set aside.

2. Brush one side of each eggplant generously with olive oil and season with salt and pepper.

3. Heat a grill pan (or BBQ) on medium-high heat.

4. Place the oiled side of each eggplant onto the pan and grill for 5-6 minutes until char marks are visible. Brush the face-up side of each eggplant with the remaining olive oil and sprinkle with salt and pepper.

5. Using tongs, turn the eggplant and cook the other side for a further 5-6 minutes until soft.

6. Transfer eggplant to a serving dish and allow to cool slightly. Then spoon yoghurt sauce on each, and scatter with coriander, mint and pomegranate seeds and, for a treat, a drizzle of honey.

GRILLED MARINATED STEAK

INGREDIENTS

5 garlic cloves, minced

1 tsp salt

¼ cup (60ml, 2fl oz) dry red wine

¼ cup (60ml, 2fl oz) balsamic vinegar

1 tbsp soy sauce

1 tbsp honey

700g (1½ lb) top round steak or flank steak

METHOD

1. Grind garlic and salt to a paste in a food processor.

2. Add red wine, balsamic vinegar, soy sauce and honey and pulse to combine.

3. Put steak a resealable plastic bag. Pour in marinade and shake to coat the meat.

4. Marinate steak in refrigerator for 4 hours or more.

5. Remove from fridge. Remove meat and bring to room temperature. Retain marinade.

6. Preheat grill to a medium-high heat. Grill the steak for 7 minutes each side, for medium-rare, or longer to your preference.

7. Let stand for 10 minutes before cutting into slices and serving, drizzled with retained marinade. Serve with chimichurri sauce (opposite).

CHIMICHURRI SAUCE

INGREDIENTS

Sauce

½ cup (10g, ½ oz) fresh coriander leaves, roughly chopped

½ cup (10g, ½ oz) fresh parsley leaves, roughly chopped

1 onion, finely chopped

½ lemon, juiced

2 tsps white wine vinegar

1 clove garlic, minced

Pinch of chilli flakes

1 tsp salt

¼ tsp pepper

⅓ cup (80ml, 3fl oz) olive oil

METHOD

1. To make the sauce, place the coriander, parsley, onion, lemon juice, vinegar, garlic, chilli flakes, salt and pepper in the bowl of a food processor and pulse until roughly chopped.

2. Slowly pour in the olive oil and process until semi-smooth. Transfer to a small bowl to serve.

MOROCCAN SPICED MINCE WITH COUSCOUS

INGREDIENTS

2 tbsps olive oil

2 onions, roughly chopped

350g (12oz) lamb mince

1 tbsp ground cumin

1 tsp ground cinnamon

2 tsps ground turmeric

100g (3½ oz) dried apricots (optional)

2½ cups (625ml, 20fl oz) vegetable stock

Extra apricots, to serve

½ cup (60g, 2oz) unsalted cashews, to serve

Couscous

1½ cups (285g, 10oz) couscous

Zest of 2 lemons

¼ cup (10g, ¼oz) mint, chopped

¼ cup (10g, ¼oz) parsley, chopped

METHOD

1. Heat oil over a medium heat in a large frying pan. Add onions and saute for 5 minutes, until soft.

2. Add mince and cook, stirring, for 5 minutes until brown. Add spices and cook for 1-2 minutes until aromatic.

3. Add apricots, if using, and stock. Stir, then reduce heat and simmer for 15 minutes.

4. Meanwhile, prepare couscous according to packet directions. When cooked, fluff with a fork and stir through the lemon zest and fresh herbs.

5. Serve mince on couscous, topped with cashew nuts and extra apricots.

SPICY MEXICAN CHILLI

INGREDIENTS

1 tbsp olive oil

1 onion, chopped

1 capsicum, finely chopped

1 red chilli, finely chopped

2 cloves garlic, minced

2 tsps dried oregano

2 tsps ground cumin

1 tsp ground cinnamon

1 tsp smoked paprika

1 tsp ground coriander

500g (1lb 2oz) beef mince

1 x 400g (14oz) can diced tomatoes

½ cup (125ml, 4fl oz) water

1 x 400g (14oz) kidney beans, drained and rinsed

Sour cream, to serve

1 tbsp coriander, finely chopped, to garnish

METHOD

1. Heat oil in a large saucepan over a medium heat. Add onion, capsicum, chilli and garlic and fry for 4 minutes.

2. Add oregano and spices and stir. Cook for 1 minute.

3. Increase heat to high. Add mince and brown for 10 minutes.

4. Add tomatoes and water. Reduce heat to a simmer and cook for 10 minutes.

5. Add kidney beans and simmer for 10 minutes, until sauce thickens.

6. Serve with sour cream and garnish with coriander.

ROASTED TURKEY WITH PEPPERCORNS

INGREDIENTS

¼ cup (40g, 1½ oz) peppercorns

1 tbsp olive oil

1 tbsp lemon juice

4 cloves garlic, minced

1 large turkey breast

METHOD

1. Preheat oven to 160°C (320°F, Gas Mark 3).

2. Grind peppercorns and olive oil in a food processor. Add lemon and garlic and pulse to combine.

3. Place turkey in a baking dish, skin side facing up.

4. Coat turkey with peppercorn marinade and rub in with fingers for 1 minute.

5. Place in the oven to roast for 45 minutes, until turkey is cooked through and golden.

6. Remove from oven and cover with foil to rest for 15 minutes before slicing.

ROASTED PORK CHOPS WITH GARLIC AND SAGE

INGREDIENTS

Salt and pepper

Olive oil

4 bone-in pork loin chops

Handful of fresh sage leaves

8 cloves garlic, halved

METHOD

1. Preheat oven to 200°C (400°F, Gas Mark 6).

2. Combine salt and pepper to taste with olive oil in a small bowl.

3. Using fingers, rub oil mixture all over the pork chops and leave to sit at room temperature for 10 minutes.

4. Heat a large frying pan over medium-high heat. Add the chops and brown on both sides, 1 to 2 minutes per side.

5. Transfer chops with pan juices to a baking dish. Press garlic into the flesh of the chops and scatter with sage leaves.

6. Place in the oven to cook for 15 minutes, until cooked through and just pink in the centre.

SERVES 6 ★ PREP 20MIN (PLUS MARINATING) ★ COOK TIME 35MIN

CHICKEN TIKKA MASALA

INGREDIENTS

12 boneless chicken thigh fillets, cut into chunks

100g (3½ oz) plain yoghurt

4 tbsps tikka masala paste

Oil, for frying

1 onion, finely chopped

1 fresh green chilli, seeded, finely chopped

3 garlic cloves, crushed

Medium piece ginger, finely grated

1 cup (250ml, 8fl oz) chicken stock

1 x 400g (14oz) can chopped tomatoes

1 tsp tomato paste

¹/₃ cup (100ml, 3fl oz) thickened cream

1 tbsp fresh lemon juice

Fresh coriander, to garnish

METHOD

1. Combine chicken, yoghurt and half the   masala paste in a bowl. Season with salt and pepper and stir to combine. Cover with plastic wrap and place in the fridge for 3 hours to marinate.

2. Heat oil in a saucepan over medium heat. Add onion, chilli, garlic and ginger and stir for 5 minutes or until onion is soft. Add the remaining curry paste and cook for 2 minutes, stirring, or until aromatic.

3. Add stock, tomatoes and tomato paste. Bring to the boil and then reduce heat to low. Simmer for 15 minutes or until sauce thickens slightly.

4. Heat oil in a large frying pan over medium heat. Sear chicken and cook for 5 minutes or until lightly browned. Add chicken to sauce and simmer for 15 minutes or until cooked through.

5. Add cream and lemon juice 5 minutes before serving and stir well to combine. Garnish with coriander to serve.

SERVES 6 ★ PREP 20MIN ★ COOK TIME 10MIN

SESAME-CRUSTED CHICKEN

METHOD

1. Cover chicken breasts with plastic wrap and gently flatten with a mallet or rolling pin until ½ cm (¼ in) thick.

2. Whisk egg whites and salt in a bowl.

3. Place sesame seeds in another bowl.

4. Dip chicken breast in egg and then in sesame seeds until well coated. Repeat until all chicken is coated.

5. Heat oil in a large frying pan over a medium heat.

6. Fry chicken for 10 minutes, turning once, until cooked through and golden. Reduce heat if browning too much.

7. Meanwhile, whisk together lemon juice, mustard and olive oil in a large bowl. Add spinach and peas and toss to coat.

8. Arrange greens on a plate and place chicken on top. Serve with fresh lemon.

INGREDIENTS

6 chicken breasts, halved

2 egg whites

1 tsp salt

1 cup (155g, 5oz) sesame seeds

⅓ cup (80ml, 3fl oz) seasame (or vegetable) oil

3 bunches of baby spinach, leaves picked

2 cups (340g, 12oz) peas

Lemon wedges, to serve

Dressing

¼ cup (60ml, 2fl oz) fresh lemon juice

1 tsp Dijon mustard

3 tsps olive oil

MEATBALLS WITH TAHINI SAUCE

INGREDIENTS

455g (1lb) lamb mince

½ onion, finely diced

2 cloves garlic, minced

Small piece ginger, minced

¼ cup (30g, 1oz) breadcrumbs

1 egg, beaten

Handful each of fresh parsley, coriander and mint leaves, finely chopped

Zest of 2 lemons

½ cup (60g, 2oz) pine nuts

½ cup (60g, 2oz) feta cheese, finely crumbled

1 tsp cinnamon

1 tsp ground cardamom

Salt and pepper

Olive oil, for frying

Juice of 1 lemon

²/3 cup (170g, 6oz) tahini

Water, as required

METHOD

1. Preheat oven to 175°C (350°F, Gas Mark 4) and line a baking tray.

2. In a large mixing bowl, combine the meat, onion, garlic, ginger, breadcrumbs, egg, fresh herbs, lemon zest, pine nuts, feta cheese, cinnamon and cardamom. Season with salt and pepper.

3. Mix well and form into small balls using your hands.

4. In batches, fry meatballs in oil in a frying pan over a medium heat until browned. Remove and place on baking tray.

5. Place in the oven and bake meatballs for 10 minutes until meat is cooked through.

6. Meanwhile, mix together the lemon juice and tahini and enough water to make a thin sauce.

7. Heat sauce over a medium to low heat until just below a simmer.

8. When meatballs are cooked and ready to serve, pour the tahini sauce on top.

9. Garnish with fresh herbs to serve.

LEMON BAKED SALMON

INGREDIENTS

4 salmon fillets,
skin removed

2 tbsps melted butter

1 lemon, juiced

2 tbsps rosemary leaves,
chopped

2 tbsps parsley, chopped

1 tbsp garlic, minced

¼ tsp mixed peppercorns

1 lemon, sliced

Black pepper

2-3 sprigs of rosemary

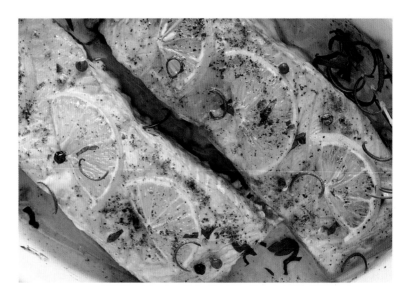

METHOD

1. Preheat oven to 205°C (400°F, Gas Mark 6) and grease a baking dish.

2. Place salmon in baking dish and brush with melted butter.

3. In a small bowl, mix together lemon juice, rosemary, parsley, garlic and peppercorns.

4. Spoon lemon mixture over the salmon.

5. Arrange lemon slices on top of salmon and grind black pepper over the top. Place rosemary sprigs in the dish.

6. Transfer to the oven and bake for 15 minutes, until cooked through.

QUINOA AND CORN BURRITOS

INGREDIENTS

1¾ cups (440ml, 15fl oz) water

1 cup (190g, 7oz) quinoa, rinsed and drained

Olive oil, for frying

½ onion, chopped

1 spring onion, sliced

3 corn cobs, kernels removed

½ tsp salt

¼ tsp pepper

1 x 400g (14oz) can black beans, drained and rinsed

½ cup (125ml, 4fl oz) chicken stock

1 tsp chilli powder

½ tsp smoked paprika

¼ tsp cayenne pepper

1 tomato, finely chopped

¼ cup (10g, ¼oz) coriander, chopped

½ lime, juiced

6 soft tortillas

METHOD

1. Bring water with a pinch of salt to a boil in a saucepan. Add quinoa, cover, and reduce heat to medium. Simmer for 15 minutes, until liquid is absorbed and quinoa is tender. Set aside.

2. Meanwhile, heat oil in a large frying pan over medium-high heat. Add onion, spring onion and corn kernels, salt and pepper and then saute for 5 minutes until onion is tender.

3. Add black beans, chicken stock, chilli powder, smoked paprika and cayenne pepper then simmer for 5 minutes, or until liquid is nearly absorbed. Add tomato then simmer for a further 2 minutes. Remove from heat and stir in coriander and lime juice. Set aside.

4. Preheat oven to 180°C (350°F, Gas Mark 4).

5. Heat tortillas according to package instructions.

6. Place open tortilla on a flat surface and place filling along one side. Roll once then tuck in sides and continue rolling to form a burrito. Wrap in foil then place in the oven to bake for 10 minutes.

DESSERTS

Lemon curd tartlets   168

Tiramisu   170

Vegan chocolate pudding   172

Green tea chia pudding   173

Blueberry pie with walnut crust   174

Vanilla cupcakes   176

Baked figs with walnuts and honey   177

Black bean brownies   178

Tropical cheesecake pots   180

Raw coconut mango balls   181

Chocolate orange cake   182

Chocolate rice pudding   184

Cocoa-dusted marzipan   185

Apple pie   186

Raw cheese cake with mixed berries   188

Peanut buttercheesecake   190

Strawberry pavlova   191

Lemon coconut bars   192

Blueberry bread trifle   194

Chickpea walnut bars   196

Vanilla cinnamon pudding   197

Chocolate rum balls   198

Marzipan plum tart   200

Paleo berry cobbler   202

Berry ice cream   203

LEMON CURD TARTLETS

INGREDIENTS

Pastry shells

2½ cups (310g, 10oz) plain flour

150g (5oz) butter

½ cup (125ml, 4fl oz) cold water

1 tbsp honey

1½ tbsps lemon zest

Lemon curd

1 cup (250ml, 8fl oz) lemon juice

2 tbsps lemon zest

⅓ cup (115g, 4oz) honey

1 cup (250ml, 8fl oz) coconut oil, melted

To serve

2 cups (200g, 7oz) blueberries

METHOD

1. Preheat oven to 190°C (375°F, Gas Mark 5). Grease four individual tart tins.

2. Sift the flour into a large bowl. Rub butter and flour together with fingertips until the mixture resembles fine breadcrumbs. Add the water, honey and lemon zest and combine until the dough just starts to come together. Bring dough together with your hands. Turn out onto a lightly floured surface and knead until smooth. Shape into a disc. Cover with plastic wrap and place in the fridge for 15 minutes.

3. Cover pastry bases with baking paper and fill with weights or rice. Place in the oven and bake for 10 minutes. Remove paper and weights and return to the oven to bake for 8 minutes or until golden. Set aside to cool completely.

4. In the meantime, place all lemon curd ingredients in a saucepan over low heat, whisking for 2-3 minutes until thickened. Set aside to cool. Place in the refrigerator to chill for 1 hour to thicken further.

5. Fill each tart shell with lemon curd. Top with berries. Serve immediately or refrigerate to serve later.

TIRAMISU

INGREDIENTS

1 tbsp instant coffee powder

1 cup (250ml, 8fl oz) hot water

250g (9oz) mascarpone

100g (3½oz) dark chocolate, melted

½ cup (125ml, 4fl oz) whipped cream

1½ tbsps brandy

2 tsps vanilla extract

6-8 sponge finger biscuits

1 tbsp cocoa powder

Extra cocoa powder, to serve

Coffee beans, to garnish

METHOD

1. Dissolve coffee in hot water.

2. Mix the mascarpone with the dark chocolate in a bowl. Fold in cream, brandy and vanilla.

3. To assemble, fill base of four serving cups with a scoop of mascarpone mixture each.

4. Dip a biscuit in coffee and then layer onto mascarpone. Continue to layer with mascarpone and coffee-dipped biscuit until cups are full.

5. Serve chilled with a dusting of cocoa powder and coffee beans.

VEGAN CHOCOLATE PUDDING

INGREDIENTS

1 ripe avocado

1½ ripe bananas

¼ cup (30g, 1oz) unsweetened cocoa powder

3 tbsps maple syrup

¼ tsp ground cinnamon

½ tsp vanilla extract

Sliced banana and chopped nuts of choice, to serve

METHOD

1. Place the avocado, banana and cocoa powder in a food processor and pulse for 1 minute until mostly smooth.

2. Still processing, gradually pour in maple syrup and blend for 1 minute. Add cinnamon and vanilla extract and blend for a further 10 seconds.

3. Scrape pudding mixture into an airtight container and refrigerate for 1 hour.

4. Spoon into serving glasses and top with sliced banana and chopped nuts.

GREEN TEA CHIA PUDDING

INGREDIENTS

2 cups (500ml, 1pt) almond milk

4 tsps honey

1 tsp culinary grade matcha

Pinch of salt

6 tbsps chia seeds

Strawberries, to finish

METHOD

1. Place almond milk, honey, matcha and salt in a jar with a secure lid and shake well to combine.

2. Place chia seeds in a bowl and pour the matcha almond milk over the top. Stir to combine and then cover with plastic wrap. Transfer to the refrigerator to chill.

3. After 15 minutes, remove from refrigerator and stir well, then return to refrigerator for 4 hours or more.

4. Serve with fresh strawberries.

BLUEBERRY PIE WITH WALNUT CRUST

INGREDIENTS

Crust

2 cups (310g, 10oz) walnuts

1 tsp bicarbonate of soda

¼ tsp salt

2 tbsps coconut oil, melted

Filling

2 tbsps cornflour

1 tbsp cold water

4 cups (400g, 14oz) fresh blueberries

2 tbsps lemon juice

1 tsp stevia

1 tsp vanilla extract

METHOD

1. Preheat oven to 175°C (350°F, Gas Mark 4).

2. Blend walnuts, bicarb and salt in a food processor until finely ground. Add coconut oil and pulse to combine.

3. Spread the crumb to line a pie dish and press firmly.

4. Transfer to the the oven to bake for 15 minutes. Remove from oven and set aside to cool.

5. Mix cornflour and water together in a small bowl to make a slurry.

6. Place blueberries, lemon juice, stevia and vanilla extract in a saucepan over a low-medium heat. Stir in cornflour slurry and simmer until sauce thickens.

7. Refrigerate for 1 hour.

8. Spoon the berry filling into the baked pie shell. Chill in fridge until ready to serve.

VANILLA CUPCAKES

INGREDIENTS

Cupcakes

150g (5oz) butter, room temperature

1½ cups (330g, 12oz) Natvia

2 eggs

2½ cups (310g, 10oz) self-raising flour

1¼ cups (310ml, 10fl oz) milk

2 tsps vanilla essence

Icing

120g (4oz) butter, room temperature

¾ cup (185ml, 6fl oz) Natvia

1 tsp vanilla extract

2 tbsps thickened cream

METHOD

1. Preheat oven to 190°C (375°F, Gas Mark 5). Place paper cases in a 12-hole muffin tray.

2. Using an electric mixer, beat butter until smooth, add Natvia and beat well until light and fluffy. Add eggs and beat. Add the sifted flour, milk and vanilla and stir until a smooth batter forms. Spoon mixture into the cases to about two-thirds full.

3. Bake for 20 minutes until golden and springy to touch. Turn out onto a wire rack to cool while you prepare the icing.

4. Place the butter and the sweetener in the bowl of an electric mixer. Beat until almost white and fluffy. Add the vanilla extract and cream. Beat until the cream has incorporated and the mixture is very fluffy. Immediately pipe onto cupcakes and serve.

SERVES 6 ★ PREP 15MIN ★ COOK TIME 20MIN

BAKED FIGS WITH WALNUTS AND HONEY

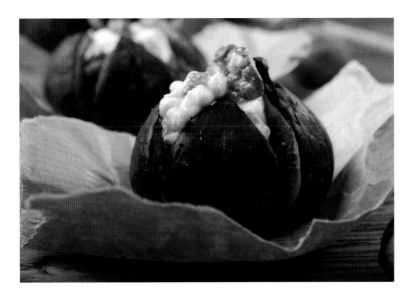

INGREDIENTS

6 ripe figs, washed and butterfly cut in quarters

1 tsp honey

½ tsp ground cloves

Candied walnuts

2 tbsps butter

2 tbsps honey

1 cup (125g, 4oz) walnuts

1 cup (225g, 8oz) goat's cheese

METHOD

1. Preheat oven to 180°C (355°F, Gas Mark 4).

2. Place the figs cut side up on a baking tray. Sprinkle with cloves and drizzle with honey.

3. Place in the oven and bake for 20 minutes.

4. Meanwhile, heat butter in a frying pan and add honey. Stir until mixture begins to bubble and caramelise. Add walnuts and stir through, coating in honey.

5. Stuff figs with goat's cheese and candied walnuts with syrup and serve warm.

BLACK BEAN BROWNIES

INGREDIENTS

1 x 400g (14oz) can
black beans

2 tbsps cocoa powder

½ cup (40g, 1½ oz)
quick oats

¼ tsp salt

⅓ cup (80ml, 3fl oz)
maple syrup

Pinch of stevia

¼ cup (60ml, 2fl oz)
coconut oil, melted

2 tsps vanilla extract

½ tsp baking powder

METHOD

1. Preheat oven to 175°C (350°F, Gas Mark 4) and grease a baking tin.

2. Combine all ingredients in a food processor and blend until smooth.

3. Spoon mixture into baking tin.

4. Place in the oven and bake for 20 minutes.

5. Allow to cool for 10 minutes before slicing.

6. Can be served immediately or stored in fridge.

TROPICAL CHEESECAKE POTS

INGREDIENTS

Crust

110g (4oz) butter, melted

16 digestive biscuits, crumbed to fine crumbs

¼ tsp stevia (optional)

Filling

1½ cups (375ml, 13fl oz) cream

450g (1lb) cream cheese, room temperature

1½ cups (375ml, 13fl oz) plain yoghurt

1 tsp liquid stevia

2 cups (500ml, 1pt) whipped cream

To serve

1 mango, diced

2 passionfruits

METHOD

1. Stir together butter and biscuit crumbs. Add stevia to sweeten, if desired.

2. Spoon 2 tablespoons of biscuit mixture into each serving cup. Set aside.

3. Beat cream on high speed until soft peaks form. Set aside.

4. In a clean bowl, beat the cream cheese, yoghurt and stevia for 2 minutes until creamy.

5. Add whipped cream and gently fold to combine.

6. Spoon cheese mix into cups.

7. Top with mango and passionfruit pulp.

SERVES 16 ★ PREP 15MIN

RAW COCONUT MANGO BALLS

INGREDIENTS

150g (5oz) dried mango

½ cup (60g, 2oz) macadamia nuts

¼ cup (60ml, 2fl oz) coconut oil

¼ cup (50g, 2oz) cacao butter

¼ cup (20g, ¾oz) desiccated coconut

½ tsp vanilla extract

¼ cup (60ml, 2fl oz) maple syrup

Water, as needed

METHOD

1. In a food processor, blend together the mango, dates, coconut oil, coconut and vanilla extract until well combined.

2. Add a spoonful of water at a time until mixture is desired texture.

3. Using hands, roll bite-sized balls from the mixture.

4. Serve immediately, or store in fridge.

CHOCOLATE ORANGE CAKE

INGREDIENTS

1 orange

½ cup (125ml, 4fl oz) maple syrup

Pinch of salt

1 tsp vanilla extract

3 eggs

2 cups (240g, 8oz) almond meal

½ cup (60g, 2oz) cocoa powder

½ tsp cinnamon

METHOD

1. Preheat oven to 165°C (330°F, Gas Mark 3). Grease and line a round cake tin with baking paper.

2. Place the orange in a saucepan of water over a medium heat and bring to the boil. Reduce heat to a gentle simmer and cover the pot. Cook the orange for 45 minutes until soft. Drain and allow to cool.

3. Roughly chop the whole orange, and then place into a food processor. Pulse until smooth.

4. Add the maple syrup, salt and vanilla extract and pulse quickly until combined. Then add eggs and pulse again.

5. Pour the mixture into a large mixing bowl. Add the almond meal, cocoa and cinnamon and mix gently with a wooden spoon just until combined.

6. Scrape the batter into the prepared tin.

7. Transfer to the oven to bake for 50 minutes until a skewer inserted in the centre comes out clean.

8. Remove from the oven and allow to cool completely in the tin.

CHOCOLATE RICE PUDDING

INGREDIENTS

180g (6oz) dark chocolate, coarsely chopped

⅓ cup (50g, 2oz) coconut sugar

1 cup (155g, 4oz) short grain rice

5 cups (1.25L, 42fl oz) water

¾ cup (185ml, 6fl oz) evapourated milk

Thickened cream and cinnamon, to serve

METHOD

1. Gently melt chocolate and sugar in a heatproof bowl over a saucepan of simmering water.

2. Stir continuously until the chocolate is completely melted and smooth and sugar has dissolved. Remove from heat. Set aside.

3. Rinse and drain rice. Transfer to a saucepan and add water. Bring to the boil. Reduce heat to low and simmer for 15 minutes, until rice is soft and liquid thickens.

4. Add melted chocolate and evapourated milk to the rice and stir through. Simmer for 3 minutes.

5. Remove from heat and allow to sit for 45 minutes.

6. Spoon into serving glasses. Serve with cream and dusted with cinnamon.

COCOA-DUSTED MARZIPAN

INGREDIENTS

2 egg whites

½ tsp stevia powder dissolved in 1 tsp hot water

2 tbsps Amaretto

2 cups (240g, 8oz) almond meal

4 tbsps unsweetened cocoa powder

METHOD

1. Place egg whites, stevia and Amaretto in the bowl of an electric mixer and beat until just combined.

2. Add the almond meal and using your hands mix together until a paste forms. It should not be sticky. If necessary add more almond meal to achieve this consistency.

3. Place the marzipan in the refrigerator to chill for 1-2 days.

4. When ready to make the marzipan balls, remove marzipan from the fridge.

5. Shake the cocoa powder onto a clean work surface or a plate.

6. Break off a piece of the marzipan and roll into a ball using your hands. Repeat until marzipan is used up.

7. Roll each marzipan ball in the cocoa.

APPLE PIE

INGREDIENTS

Filling

10 apples, peeled, cored and sliced

½ cup (125ml, 4fl oz) apple juice (or water)

2 tsps vanilla extract

1 tsp cinnamon

1 tbsp maple syrup

Pastry

2½ cups (310g, 10oz) wholemeal spelt flour

½ tsp salt

200g (7oz) butter, chilled, diced

1-3 tbsp cold water

METHOD

1. Place the apples, apple juice, vanilla extract and cinnamon in a large saucepan over a medium-high heat.

2. Cook, stirring occasionally, for 15 minutes until apples are soft and tender.

3. Add the maple syrup. Stir, then set aside to cool.

4. Combine the spelt flour, salt and butter in the bowl of a food processor. Pulse lightly until the mixture resembles fine breadcrumbs. Gradually add water and bring the dough together with your hands. You may not need to add all the water.

5. Form the pastry dough into a disc and cover with plastic wrap. Transfer to the fridge to chill for 30 minutes.

6. Preheat the oven to 180°C (350°F, Gas Mark 4) and grease an ovenproof pie dish.

7. Remove the pastry from the fridge and separate into one-third and two-thirds pieces.

8. Roll out the larger ball to fit the base and sides of the pie dish. Push pastry into the base of the dish and up the sides. Trim off the edges of the pastry.

9. Spoon the apple filling into the dish.

10. Roll out the rest of the pastry and gently place over the top. Seal edges by pressing down gently.

11. Transfer to the oven and bake for 35 minutes or until golden.

RAW CHEESECAKE WITH MIXED BERRIES

INGREDIENTS

Crust

1½ cups (185g, 6oz) almonds

1 pinch salt

½ cup (80g, 3oz) dates

¼ cup (20g, ¾ oz) dried, unsweetened coconut

Filling

3 cups (375g, 12oz) cashews

¾ cup (185ml, 6fl oz) lemon juice

¾ cup (260g, 9oz) honey

¾ cup (185ml, 6fl oz) coconut oil

1 tbsp vanilla extract

Water, as required

Topping

2 cups (400g, 14oz) strawberries, frozen

1 cup (200g, 7oz) mixed berries, frozen

METHOD

1. Place almonds, salt and dates into a food processor and pulse until well combined and rough in texture.

2. Sprinkle the coconut onto the bottom of a round cake tin, then press the almond and date mixture down into the pan to form the crust.

3. Place filling ingredients into a blender and pulse, adding water only if needed to loosen the mixture for blending. Spoon mixture on top of crust.

4. Place the dish in the freezer for 1 hour.

5. Place strawberries into the blender and pulse until smooth. Pour this mixture on top of the middle layer.

6. Place the raw cake back in freezer and freeze for 5 hours.

7. Defrost 30 minutes before serving. Decorate with frozen mixed berries to serve.

PEANUT BUTTER CHEESECAKE

INGREDIENTS

Ginger snap crust

30 sugar-free ginger snap cookies

½ cup (60g, 2oz) peanuts

5 tbsps butter, melted

Topping

450g (1lb) cream cheese, softened

1½ cups 375g (13oz) sugar-free smooth peanut butter

Pinch of stevia (optional)

½ cup (125ml, 4fl oz) sour cream

½ cup (125ml, 4fl oz) thickened cream

Handful peanuts, to serve

Sprig mint, to garnish

METHOD

1. Place cookies and peanuts in a blender and process until a rough crumb forms. Pour into a bowl, add butter, and stir to combine.

2. Press cookie mixture into the base of a greased cake tin. Refrigerate for 1 hour.

3. Using an electric mixer, beat cream cheese, peanut butter and stevia, if using, together.

4. Add sour cream and thickened cream and mix until smooth.

5. Pour cream mix onto cookie base. Refrigerate for 3 hours.

6. Serve cool, topped with a few peanuts and mint.

STRAWBERRY PAVLOVA

INGREDIENTS

6 egg whites

Pinch of salt

1½ tsps liquid stevia

3 tsps cornflour

1 tsp vanilla extract

1½ tsps white
or malt vinegar

2 cups (400g, 14oz)
strawberries, quartered

METHOD

1. Preheat oven to 120°C (250°F, Gas Mark ½).

2. Wet baking paper before lining a baking tray.

3. Place eggwhites and salt into the bowl of an electric mixer
   and beat until stiff peaks form.

4. Add stevia, cornflour, vanilla and vinegar and beat quickly
   to combine.

5. Scrape mixture onto baking tray, forming into a circle using
   a spatula.

6. Place in the oven and bake for 1 hour until cooked.

7. Allow to cool before topping with strawberries.

LEMON COCONUT BARS

INGREDIENTS

Base

¾ cups (260g, 9oz) honey

½ cup (125ml, 4fl oz) coconut oil, room temperature

Pinch of salt

¾ cup (60g, 2oz) desiccated coconut

1 cup (125g, 4oz) coconut flour, sifted

Filling

3 eggs

½ cup (180g, 6oz) honey

Zest of 1 lemon

2 tsps coconut flour

Juice of 3 lemons

METHOD

1. Preheat oven to 175°C (350°F, Gas Mark 4). Grease a rectangular baking tin.

2. In an electric mixer, beat together honey, coconut oil and salt until creamy. Add desiccated coconut and mix until well combined.

3. Fold in coconut flour until a soft dough forms.

4. Press dough into the cake tin. Place in the oven and bake for 8 minutes, until golden brown. Remove from oven and allow to cool for 30 minutes.

5. Lower oven temperature to 160°C (320°F, Gas Mark 3).

6. In a clean bowl, using the electric mixer whisk the eggs, honey and lemon zest together.

7. In another bowl, combine the coconut flour and lemon juice.

8. Add the egg mixture into the flour mixture and fold to incorporate.

9. Pour lemon filling over the baked crust and return to the oven to bake for 20 minutes, until set.

10. Remove from oven and set aside to cool partially. Cover and refrigerate for 6 hours. When chilled, slice into bars.

BLUEBERRY BREAD TRIFLE

INGREDIENTS

½ cup (110g, 4oz) mascarpone cheese

3 cups (750ml, 24fl oz) milk

2 tsps vanilla extract

Zest of 1 lemon

1 tsp fresh lemon juice

3 tbsps butter, melted

450g (1lb) bread, crusts removed and cut into chunks

¾ cup (185ml, 6fl oz) cream

2 tsps rice malt syrup

1 cup (250ml, 8fl oz) low-sugar vanilla custard

3 fresh apricots, peeled and sliced

1½ cups (150g, 5oz) blueberries

Mint leaves, to garnish

METHOD

1. Make ready 6 glass jars or serving dishes.

2. Using an electric mixer, beat the mascarpone, milk, vanilla, lemon zest and lemon juice until combined. Pour in butter and stir well to fully combine.

3. Place bread cubes in a shallow dish and pour mixture over the top, ensuring it covers the bread completely. Set aside to absorb for 20 minutes.

4. Combine cream and rice malt syrup in a bowl.

5. Assemble the pudding, starting with a layer of bread mixture, then add custard and sweetened cream, then top with apricots and blueberries.

CHICKPEA WALNUT BARS

INGREDIENTS

1 x 400g (14oz) can
chickpeas, rinsed and drained

½ cup (125g, 4oz)
nut butter

⅓ cup (80ml, 3fl oz)
maple syrup

2 tbsps ground flaxseed

1 tsp vanilla extract

½ tsp salt

½ tsp baking powder

¼ tsp bicarbonate of soda

⅓ cup (40g, 1½ oz)
walnuts, finely chopped

METHOD

1. Preheat the oven to 180°C (355°F, Gas Mark 4) and line a deep-sided baking tray.

2. Place all ingredients into a food processor and combine until a rough batter forms.

3. Spread the batter into the baking tray.

4. Place in the oven and bake for 25-30 minutes or until a skewer inserted in the centre comes out clean.

5. Remove from oven and allow to cool completely in the tin on a wire rack.

6. Place in the fridge to set for 1 hour or more before slicing into bars.

VANILLA CINNAMON PUDDING

INGREDIENTS

2 cups (500ml, 1pt) almond milk

6 egg yolks

110g (4oz) powdered erythritol

⅓ cup (50g, 2oz) cornflour

1 tsp vanilla extract

2 tsps cinammon

METHOD

1. Place all of ingredients in a large mixing bowl and whisk to combine.

2. Pour into a large saucepan over medium-low heat. Cook, stirring constantly, until mixture starts to thicken.

3. When mixture reaches a pudding-like consistency, remove from the heat and whisk vigorously to eliminate clumps and aerate.

4. Pour into serving glasses and cover with plastic wrap. Ensure wrap touches the pudding to avoid moisture build up.

5. Refrigerate for 4 hours before serving decorated with mint and cinammon.

CHOCOLATE RUM BALLS

INGREDIENTS

225g (8oz, ½ lb)
almond butter

2 tsps rum extract

3 tbsps unsweetened
cocoa powder

½ cup (125ml, 4fl oz)
powdered erythritol

¾ cup (60g, 2oz)
desiccated coconut

METHOD

1. Place the almond butter and rum extract in a medium bowl. Sift in the cocoa powder and powdered erythritol.

2. Bring the mixture together with your hands, kneading until it is smooth and thoroughly combined.

3. Make ready a baking tray or plate that will fit into your freezer. Line with baking paper.

4. Roll mixture into small balls and place on the tray. Transfer to the freezer for 2 hours.

5. Remove the balls from the freezer and roll each in desiccated coconut to serve.

MARZIPAN PLUM TART

INGREDIENTS

Marzipan

1¼ cups (155g, 5oz) almond flour

100g (3½ oz) powdered erythritol

1 egg white

½ tsp almond extract

Base

4 sheets of shortcrust pastry, defrosted

1 egg, beaten

Filling

3 tbsps double cream

4 white plums, sliced

2 tbsps honey

Garnish

¼ cup (30g, 1oz) pistachio nuts, chopped

¼ cup powdered erythritol

½ tsp cornflour

METHOD

1. Preheat oven to 200°C (390°F, Gas Mark 6). Line an oblong cake tin with greaseproof paper.

2. To make the marzipan, sift the almond flour and powdered erythritol over a medium bowl. Add the egg white and almond extract and mix until a rough paste forms. Knead for 1 minute until smooth. Form into a ball. Wrap in plastic wrap and set aside.

3. Press pastry into tin. Transfer to the oven and blind bake with weights for 15 minutes.

4. Remove weights. Brush pastry base with beaten egg and return to oven to bake for a further 10 minutes. Remove from oven and set aside to cool slightly.

5. Meanwhile, combine the marzipan and cream until smooth and then spoon filling onto pastry base.

6. Arrange plum slices standing in marzipan, skin facing up. Drizzle with honey.

7. Return to oven to bake for 30 minutes, until golden.

8. Process erythritol and cornflour in a food processor until it is the consistency of icing sugar. Sprinkle tart with erythritol mixture and pistachios.

PALEO BERRY COBBLER

INGREDIENTS

3 cups (400g, 14oz)
fresh berries

1 egg, beaten

1½ cups (180g, 6oz)
almond meal

¼ cup (30g, 1oz) walnuts,
chopped

2 tbsps coconut oil

½ tsp cinnamon

1 tbsp honey

Coconut milk, to serve

METHOD

1. Preheat oven to 175°C (350°F, Gas Mark 4).

2. Place berries in a greased ovenproof dish. Set aside.

3. Combine egg, almond meal, walnuts, coconut oil and cinnamon
    together in a large mixing bowl and stir to combine. Rub with
    fingertips to form a crumble.

4. Drizzle honey on top of the berries and scatter crumble on top.

5. Place in the oven and bake for 35 minutes, until golden and crunchy.

6. Serve with coconut milk.

SERVES 4 ★ PREP 20MIN (PLUS FREEZING)

BERRY ICE CREAM

INGREDIENTS

3 cups (400g, 14oz)
mixed frozen berries

Zest of 1 lemon

Pinch of stevia, optional

1½ cups coconut milk

Handful of frozen berries,
to garnish

METHOD

1. Place all the ingredients in a blender and process until smooth and creamy. Transfer to a freezer-safe container.

2. Place in the freezer for 4 hours.

3. Remove from the freezer. Break up the mixture and return it to the blender and process again until soft.

4. Return to the freezer for a further 2 hours and then blend again.

5. Return to the freezer for a further 1 hour and blend again. This time, return to the refrigerator and allow to chill for 30 minutes before serving.

6. Serve topped with frozen berries.

DRINKS

Purple bliss smoothie   206
Wake up smoothie   208
Get up and go smoothie   209
Lemon-mint ice tea   210
Matcha smoothie   211
Iced coffee   212
Green smoothie   214
Cucumber mint cooler   215
Sweet cream smoothie   216
Kiwi kick start smoothie   217
Blueberry lemonade   218
Dairy-free berry smoothie   220
Turmeric spiced milk   221

PURPLE BLISS SMOOTHIE

INGREDIENTS

2 cups (200g, 7oz)
blueberries
(fresh or frozen)

1 cup (125g, 4oz)
raspberries
(fresh or frozen)

1 banana
(fresh or frozen)

2 tbsps chia seeds

½ beetroot, peeled
and diced

1 cup (250ml, 8fl oz)
coconut water

Ice cubes, as needed

1 tsp rice malt syrup
(optional)

Freshly grated coconut,
to garnish

METHOD

1. Place blueberries, raspberries, banana, chia seeds and beetroot in a blender and pulse for 30 seconds until pulverised.

2. Add coconut water. Continue blending until smooth.

3. Blend in ice for texture as required if not using frozen fruit.

4. Add rice malt syrup for sweetening, if required.

5. Garnish with grated coconut.

WAKE UP SMOOTHIE

INGREDIENTS

4 large carrots, chopped

1½ cups (375ml, 13fl oz) water

1 frozen banana, sliced

1 tbsp chopped ginger

Juice of 1 lemon

1 cup (250ml, 8fl oz) almond milk

METHOD

1. Blend the carrots and water on high speed until pureed.

2. Strain out carrot pulp and retain juice.

3. Blend carrot juice, banana, ginger, lemon juice and almond milk until smooth.

GET UP AND GO SMOOTHIE

INGREDIENTS

2 apples, cored and quartered

1 ripe avocado

Water, as needed

Ice cubes, to chill

Sprig mint, to garnish

METHOD

1. Blend the apple pieces and avocado on a high speed, gradually adding water to achieve desired thickness.

2. Continue to blend until creamy and smooth.

3. Serve cool, with ice cubes if desired.

4. Garnish with mint leaves

LEMON-MINT ICE TEA

INGREDIENTS

1 lemon, sliced thinly

12 fresh mint leaves, plus a few to garnish

3 cups (750ml, 24fl oz) of tea, chilled

Ice cubes, to serve

METHOD

1. Divide lemon and mint between two tall glasses.

2. Pour in cool tea and stir.

3. Add a few ice cubes.

4. Refrigerate for up to 6 hours before serving.

5. Serve garnished with mint.

MATCHA SMOOTHIE

INGREDIENTS

½ cup (115g, 4oz) yoghurt, plus extra to serve

2 tbsps honey

Handful of ice cubes

1 tsp culinary grade matcha

METHOD

1. Place ingredients in a blender and pulse until well combined and slightly frothy.

2. Serve chilled with extra yoghurt and matcha, to garnish.

ICED COFFEE

INGREDIENTS

⅓ cup (60g, 2oz) freshly ground coffee

1½ cups (375ml, 13fl oz) cold water

Ice, to taste

Milk, to taste

1 tsp rice malt syrup, to taste

METHOD

1. Place coffee and water in a plunger.

2. Leave to steep in the fridge overnight with plunger in upright position.

3. When ready to drink, remove from fridge. Plunge coffee to separate liquid from grounds.

4. Fill two large glasses with ice cubes. Pour coffee over the ice and add milk, to taste.

5. For a sweeter version, add rice malt syrup.

GREEN SMOOTHIE

INGREDIENTS

1 small ripe banana

1 cup milk

1 large handful spinach leaves

6-8 almonds

½ cup (75g, 3oz) ice cubes

METHOD

1. Blend ingredients together until well combined and smooth.

2. Add ice and blend.

3. Serve immediately.

SERVES 2 ★ PREP 5MIN

CUCUMBER MINT COOLER

INGREDIENTS

1 cucumber, thinly sliced

4 slices of lime

4 large sprigs of mint, plus extra to garnish

3½ cups (875ml, 30fl oz) water

METHOD

1. Muddle the cucumber, lime and mint in a serving jug.

2. Add water and stir until well combined.

3. Serve over ice. Garnish with extra mint.

SWEET CREAM SMOOTHIE

INGREDIENTS

2 tbsps rolled oats, uncooked

1 cup (250ml, 8fl oz) almond milk

½ tsp vanilla extract

1 frozen banana, sliced

1 tbsp almond butter

1 tsp rice malt syrup

1 tbsp soaked chia seeds

1 tsp maca powder (optional)

Sprinkle of rolled oats, to garnish

METHOD

1. Soak the rolled oats in enough boiling water to just cover. Set aside for 15 minutes, until soft.

2. Place all ingredients in a blender and pulse on high speed until creamy.

3. Serve in a tall glass with a sprinkle of oats on top

KIWI KICK-START SMOOTHIE

INGREDIENTS

1 cup (250ml, 8fl oz) water

Juice of 1 lime

2 kiwi fruit, sliced

1 frozen banana, sliced

1 large cucumber, sliced

METHOD

1. Add water and lime juice to blender, then add fruit and cucumber.

2. Blend on high for 30 seconds, until smooth and creamy.

BLUEBERRY LEMONADE

INGREDIENTS

4 lemons, juiced

3 cups (300g, 10oz)
fresh blueberries

Pinch of stevia

4 cups (1L, 2pt) water

Ice cubes, to serve

Extra berries, to garnish

Lemon slice, garnish

METHOD

1. Place lemon juice, blueberries, stevia and water in a blender and pulse on high for 10 seconds, until smooth.

2. Strain out pulp and retain juice.

3. Serve chilled, or poured over ice cubes.

4. Top with a few berries and lemon slice.

DAIRY-FREE BERRY SMOOTHIE

INGREDIENTS

1 cup (250ml, 8fl oz) almond milk

½ frozen banana

¼ cup (20g, ¾ oz) rolled oats

2 tbsps raw almonds

½ tsp stevia

1 cup (100g, 3½ oz) frozen blueberries

Extra blueberries, to garnish

Few mint leaves, to garnish

METHOD

1. Blend all ingredients except garnish together on high for 10 seconds, then medium-high for further 40 seconds until well combined and creamy.

2. Serve topped with berries and garnished with a mint leaf.

SERVES 1 ★ PREP 5MIN ★ COOK TIME 5MIN

TURMERIC SPICED MILK

INGREDIENTS

1 cup (250ml, 8fl oz) coconut milk

½ tsp turmeric

¼ tsp black pepper

1 cinnamon quill

1 cardamom pod

½ tsp coconut oil

Honey, to taste

METHOD

1. Pour milk into a saucepan over a low-medium heat.

2. Add turmeric, pepper and cinnamon quill and stir through.

3. Meanwhile, crush seeds from cardamom pod.

4. Add cardamom seeds and coconut oil.

5. Bring turmeric milk to the boil, then simmer for 3 minutes.

6. Strain before serving.

7. Sweeten with honey, to taste.

.

INDEX

almonds
almond-crusted chicken tenders 137
cocoa-dusted marzipan 185
raw cheesecake with berries 188
sweet cream smoothie 216
apple
apple pie 186
get up and go smoothie 209
red quinoa with apples 28
asparagus
asparagus frittata 23
asparagus tart 99
avocado
avocado hummus 113
avocado scrambled egg wraps 19
egg baked in avocado 30
get up and go smoothie 209
vegan chocolate pudding 172
bacon
potato salad with crispy bacon 77
warm salad of beans and bacon 60
banana
green smoothie 214
protein muffins 22
sweet cream smoothie 216
barley
bean and barley salad bowl 46
warm chicken salad 68
beans
bean and barley salad bowl 46
black bean brownies 178
black bean dip 103
broad bean patties 112
broad bean salad 64
eggplant and white bean balls 144
green goddess soup 73
parsley and three bean salad 44
spicy Mexican chilli 156
spring rice salad 49
the business burgers 83
walnut and bean salad 57
warm salad of beans and bacon 60
beef
beef soba noodles 96
grilled marinated steak 152
meatloaf with honey glaze 148
Moroccan mince with couscous 154
spicy Mexican chilli 156
beetroot
chocolate and beetroot muffins 118
orange, pistachio, beetroot salad 50
purple bliss smoothie 206
roast beetroot salad with dukkah 76
zesty warm chicken salad 66
berries
berry ice cream 203
blueberry bread trifle 194

blueberry lemonade 218
blueberry pie with walnut crust 174
blueberry yoghurt pot 34
chia berry pots with lavender honey 20
dairy-free berry smoothie 220
Paleo berry cobbler 202
purple bliss smoothie 206
quinoa porridge bowl 38
raw cheesecake with berries 188
strawberry pavlova 191
whole wheat blackberry pancakes 32
bone broth 65
broccoli
broccoli and corn quesadilla 95
Brussels sprouts
sprouts with pork and peanuts 126
carrot
wake up smoothie 208
cashews
cashew oat bars 116
coco-cashew nut butter 31
raw cheesecake with berries 188
cauliflower
cauliflower rice 129
cheese, *see also* **cream cheese**
cheesy zucchini bread 84
feta and spinach pancakes 106
gluten-free pizza 86
nourishing quinoa and feta salad 62
rye galette with ricotta 92
stuffed omelette 13
chia
chia berry pots with lavender honey 20
coconut mango chia pudding 12
gluten-free pizza 86
green tea chia pudding 173
quinoa porridge bowl 38
wholesome nut and seed loaf 94
chicken
almond-crusted chicken tenders 137
baked chicken rolls 138
Bombay chicken and potatoes 136
chicken frittata 110
chicken noodle miso bowl 54
chicken tikka masala 160
coconut and lime chicken 147
sesame-crusted chicken 161
sesame miso chicken 58
warm chicken salad 68
zesty warm chicken salad 66
chickpeas
avocado hummus 113
chickpea walnut bars 196
chilli
spicy Mexican chilli 156
chimichurri sauce 153
chocolate
black bean brownies 178

chocolate and beetroot muffins 118
chocolate orange cake 182
chocolate rice pudding 184
chocolate rum balls 198
date, nut and chocolate bars 114
peanut butter choc bars 122
tiramisu 170
vegan chocolate pudding 172
cinnamon
cinnamon rice porridge 39
vanilla cinnamon pudding 197
coconut
coco-cashew nut butter 31
coconut and lime chicken 147
coconut mango chia pudding 12
coconut mango rice pudding 26
coconut prawn curry 140
lemon coconut bars 192
raw coconut mango balls 181
coffee
iced coffee 212
tiramisu 170
corn
broccoli and corn quesadilla 95
quinoa and corn burritos 165
couscous
Moroccan mince with couscous 154
cream cheese
peanut butter cheesecake 190
tropical cheesecake pots 180
cucumber
cucumber mint cooler 215
kiwi kick-start smoothie 217
dates
date, nut and chocolate bars 114
sesame date bliss balls 120
egg
asparagus frittata 23
avocado scrambled egg wraps 19
chicken frittata 110
egg baked in avocado 30
florentine eggs 36
hearty quinoa with baked eggs 10
homemade mayonnaise 61
omelette with mushrooms 24
poached egg with spinach 40
quinoa fritters with eggs 108
stuffed omelette 13
eggplant
eggplant and white bean balls 144
grilled eggplant 150
nourishing quinoa and feta salad 62
fig
baked figs with walnuts and
        honey 177
fish
easy seafood chowder 69

fish with lemon and thyme 130
grilled salmon with tartare sauce 128
grilled sardines with lemon 27
lemon baked salmon 164

ginger
glazed ginger prawns 70
wake up smoothie 208

hazelnuts
wholesome nut and seed loaf 94

kale
kale chips 87
sweet kale salad 72

kiwi fruit
kiwi kick-start smoothie 217

lamb
meatballs with tahini sauce 162
Moroccan mince with couscous 154
spiced lamb cutlets 146

lemon
blueberry lemonade 218
fish with lemon and thyme 130
lemon and lime cake 121
lemon baked salmon 164
lemon coconut bars 192
lemon curd tartlets 168
lemon dill coleslaw 143
lemon-mint ice tea 210
rosemary and lemon dressing 45

lentils
red lentil soup 48
spicy sausage, lentil and tomato
    soup 74

lime
coconut and lime chicken 147
lemon and lime cake 121
lime rice salad 142

mango
coconut mango chia pudding 12
coconut mango rice pudding 26
raw mango coconut balls 181

marzipan
cocoa-dusted marzipan 185
marzipan plum tart 200

matcha
green tea chia pudding 173
matcha smoothie 211

mayonnaise 61
millet
savoury millet porridge 107
the business burgers 83

miso
chicken noodle miso bowl 54
miso with udon noodles 53
sesame miso chicken 58

mushrooms
baked chicken rolls 138
gluten-free pizza 86
miso with udon noodles 53
omelette with mushrooms 24
rye galette with mushrooms 92

noodles
beef soba noodles 96

chicken noodle miso bowl 54
miso with udon noodles 53

oats
cashew oat bars 116
homemade granola 14
overnight oatmeal 35
power nutbread 90
pumpkin oat cookies 117
sweet cream smoothie 216
whole wheat blackberry pancakes 32

orange
chocolate orange cake 182
orange, pistachio, beetroot salad 50
zesty warm chicken salad 66

pasta
prawns with spaghetti and pistachio
    pesto 132

peanut butter
peanut butter bars 122
peanut butter cheesecake 190
peanut butter cookies 91

peanuts
sprouts with pork and peanuts 126

peas
green goddess soup 73
green pea fritters 102
simple pea soup 52

pistachios
orange, pistachio, beetroot salad 50
prawns with spaghetti and pistachio
    pesto 132

plum
marzipan plum tart 200

pork
meatballs with zucchini pasta 134
roasted pork chops with garlic and
    sage 158
sprouts with pork and peanuts 126

potato
Bombay chicken and potatoes 136
potato salad with crispy bacon 77

pumpkin
classic pumpkin soup 56
pumpkin oat cookies 117
the business burgers 83

quinoa
asparagus frittata 23
hearty quinoa with baked eggs 10
nourishing quinoa and feta salad 62
quinoa and corn burritos 165
quinoa fritters with eggs 108
quinoa porridge bowl 38
red quinoa with apples 28

rice
chocolate rice pudding 184
cinnamon rice porridge 39
lime rice salad 142
spring rice salad 49

rosemary
rosemary and lemon dressing 45

sausage
spicy sausage, lentil and tomato
    soup 74

seafood
coconut prawn curry 140

easy seafood chowder 69
glazed ginger prawns 70
prawns with spaghetti and pistachio
    pesto 132
steamed mussels in white wine sauce 104

sesame
flax and sesame seed crackers 100
sesame-crusted chicken 161
sesame date bliss balls 120
sesame miso chicken 58
tahini dressing 98

spinach
feta and spinach pancakes 106
florentine eggs 36
green smoothie 214
poached egg with spinach 40
stuffed omelette 13

tahini
meatballs with tahini sauce 162
tahini dressing 98

tea
green tea chia pudding 173
lemon-mint ice tea 210
matcha smoothie 211

tofu
scrambled tofu on toast 16

tomato
roasted fennel cherry tomatoes 18
scrambled tofu on toast 16
spicy sausage, lentil and tomato
    soup 74
sun-dried tomato tart 88

turkey
roasted turkey with peppercorns 157
smoked turkey and vegetable tarts 80

turmeric
turmeric spiced milk 221

vanilla
vanilla cinnamon pudding 197
vanilla cupcakes 176

walnuts
baked figs with walnuts and
    honey 177
blueberry pie with walnut crust 174
chickpea walnut bars 196
date, nut and chocolate bars 114
power nutbread 90
walnut and bean salad 57

yoghurt
blueberry yoghurt pot 34
zucchini fries with chive yoghurt
    dip 133

zucchini
broccoli and corn quesadilla 95
cheesy zucchini bread 84
meatballs with zucchini pasta 134
spring rice salad 49
zucchini fries with chive yoghurt
    dip 133
zucchini fritters 82

HERRON
book distributors

First Published in 2016 by Herron Book Distributors Pty Ltd
14 Manton St
Morningside
QLD 4170
www.herronbooks.com

WWW.CAPTAINHONEY.COM.AU

Custom book production by Captain Honey Pty Ltd
12 Station St
Bangalow
NSW 2479
www.captainhoney.com.au

Cataloguing-in-Publication. A catalogue record for this book is available from the National Library of Australia

ISBN 978-0-947163-13-6

Printed and bound in China by 1010 Printing International Limited

5 4   19 20

NOTES FOR THE READER

Preparation, cooking times and serving sizes vary according to the skill, agility and appetite of the cook and should be used as a guide only.

All reasonable efforts have been made to ensure the accuracy of the content in this book. Information in this book is not intended as a substitute for medical advice. The author and publisher cannot and do not accept any legal duty of care or responsibility in relation to the content in this book, and disclaim any liabilities relating to its use.

PHOTO CREDITS

Front cover: Anna Shepulova
Back cover: Anna Shepulova
5PH p248. Alena Haurylik p61, 73. alexpro9500 p157, 171. AnastasiaKopa p69. Anna Hoychuk p67, 219, 223, 234. Anna Shepulova p113, 119, 185, 197. Antonova Anna p161. BGSmith p176. bitt24 p241. Brent Hofacker p33, 153. Dani Vincek p29. Elena M. Tarasova p121. Elena Shashkina p205, 221. Elena Veselova p98, 111, 229. Foodio p187. Goode Imaging p74. gresei p53. hadasit p169. HandmadePictures p225. hlphoto p149. holbox p249. Ildi Papp p23, 66, 231. Innershadows Photography p211. istetiana p15. its_al_dente p58. iuliia_n p252. Ivanna Grigorova p213. JeniFoto p37. Joe Gough p14. Joshua Resnick p187. Josie Grant p179. Kamila i Wojtek Cyganek p177. Karpenkov Denis p39. Kati Molin p19. kostrez p44. Lecic p246. Liliya Kandrashevich p17. Liljam p227. Lisovskaya Natalia p168. Liv friis-larsen p235. Louno Morose p243. Lukas Gojda p89. Magdanatka p127. mama_mia p22. MangoRicePudding_227623540_Elena Veselova.jpg p28. MaraZe p103. marysckin p65. Maxsol p36. Natalie_Barth p105. Nataliya Arzamasova p11, 13, 45, 51, 52, 55, 63, 93, 99, 104, 107, 117, 122, 123, 125, 129, 131, 135, 137, 141, 143, 160, 163, 167, 173, 175, 181, 191, 202, 203, 207, 215, 220, 226, 239, 251. Natasha Breen p43. natashamam p201. Nitr p242. Olena Kaminetska p247. Olga Markova p85, 136. Olga Nayashkova p152. Peter O'Toole p217. Ravil Sayfullin p240. s_karau p41. saschanti17 p21. Shebeko p87. Simone van den Berg p233. Stepanek Photography p25. Stephanie Frey p31, 133. Stolyevych Yuliya p59. Teresa Kasprzycka p130, 209. TGTGTG p2. Timolina p57, 79, 155, 193. tiverylucky p115. topotishka p139, 147. vanillaechoes p75, 77, 165. viennetta p245. vm2002 p183. Yuliya Gontar p8, 46, 90, 144, 194, 236
Images used under license from Shutterstock.com